BLADE's
GUIDE TO
BUYING
KNIVES

JASON FRY
FOREWORD BY STEVE SHACKLEFORD

Published by

Gun Digest® Books, an imprint of Caribou Media Group, LLC
Gun Digest Media
5600 W. Grande Market Drive, Suite 100
Appleton, WI 54913
gundigest.com

To order books or other products call 920.471.4522 ext. 104
or visit us online at gundigeststore.com

ISBN-13: 9781951115685

Edited by Ben Sobieck and Corey Graff
Designed by Jong Cadelina
Cover design by Gene Coo
Presto knife cover image courtesy of Arizona Custom Knives

Printed in the United States of America

10 9 8 7 6 5 4 3 2 1

CONTENTS

FOREWORD

Before you buy the knives that appeal to you, wouldn't it also make sense if you could determine with a degree of certainty how they rate in terms of quality, construction, materials, value and other key areas? A good way to do that is to study this book.

As an award-winning knifemaker, author Jason Fry brings a skill set to the equation most non-knifemakers do not: he knows how knives should be made and, perhaps more importantly, how they should *not*.

First and foremost, a knife must cut and cut well. Its cutting ability depends on several things, including the type and quality of the blade's steel, its heat treatment and grind/geometry, the design of the handle and more. Jason covers it all, as well as the many steel types, the elements in each type, whether the blade is forged or fashioned mostly by stock removal, and so on.

Before you can buy knives intelligently, you need to know the styles, patterns and types, and you need to know exactly what they are and what they're designed for. Moreover, are they custom/handmade or factory/production? Jason has your "6" on these subjects, too.

As with most collectibles, the looks of a knife are key. The author explains the many different handle materials and blade finishes that play a large role in a knife's aesthetics. And if the knife folds, what kind of mechanism does it use? Does it lock or not?

Quality construction plays a pivotal role in a knife's desirability. Jason schools you on how to recognize proper *fit and finish*—where each side of the knife matches the other, the backspring of a slipjoint fits tight with no gaps between it and the blade tang when the knife is open, etc. Jason nails it all.

One key to the custom side of knife buying is the personality and reputation of the maker. Many collect the knives of just one maker or of a select few makers based not only on knife quality but also the "cool factor" of the maker himself/herself. Jason outlines these all-important considerations.

Learning *how* to buy is almost as important as *what* to buy. One way is to attend knife shows to see and handle the knives yourself. This way you get to meet the makers and also the professionals—the dealers/purveyors—who act as the middlemen. Jason covers buying knives on the web, eBay, forums, social media, at retail knife stores and elsewhere, including how to get the most for your money and how to keep from getting burned.

The author breaks the collector down into categories as well. You might fit one or more of the categories—or you might just fit into your own category. It's good to know the types of collectors and the knives they collect so you can optimize your ability to buy from and sell to them, too.

As with all collectibles, knives have their own language/nomenclature. *Choil, ricasso, plunge, spine, swedge, quillon, bolster* and more are all knife features you need to understand. Once you finish this book, you'll be able to talk knife-ese with makers, collectors, dealers and the sharpest blade geeks anywhere.

There's much more—including mid-tech knives, low- to higher-end pieces, knife maintenance tips, history, etc. Read it, re-read it and keep it handy as a reference. It's a sure way to ensure you buy and collect the best knives, which helps guarantee you enjoy yourself in the process. And isn't enjoyment much of what it's all about? ▲

Steve Shackleford
Editor, *BLADE*® Magazine

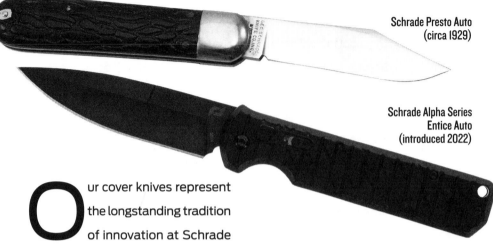

Schrade Presto Auto
(circa 1929)

Schrade Alpha Series
Entice Auto
(introduced 2022)

O ur cover knives represent the longstanding tradition of innovation at Schrade Knives, a company with a remarkable 130-year history. The Presto is an original George Schrade design and was introduced in 1929. The Entice Auto, introduced in 2022, marks the start of a new era at Schrade and is one of several models in the company's new Made-in-USA Alpha Series.

History of Schrade

In 1892, George Schrade patented a press-button switchblade. Nearing the turn of the 20th century, before Hollywood depictions of switchblades — also known as "Automatics" — would cast them as the tools of villains or organized crime bosses, the design was purely practical.

"The United States led production and distribution of automatic knives for most of the early 20th century, boosted by George Schrade and the onset of mass production," notes Zach Whitmore in "Why Switchblades Are Illegal," writing for BLADE Magazine.

"Schrade set up shops all over the country as well as abroad. Schrade produced and advertised automatic knives mostly to and for ranchers, outdoorsmen, hunters, and farmers as quick, one-handed utility tools. Business was good, and people liked their snappy, modern Presto pocket-knives."

In addition to its automatically deployable blade, the Presto was an attractive piece characterized by either plastic or hand-picked bone handles. The blade was typically 4-1/8 inches tip to tang; the overall length was 8-3/4 inches.

Re-Introduction of U.S-Made Products

The Entice shown on our cover is an out-the-side automatic with a push-button open and plunge lock sporting a 3.5-inch S35VN black-coated bayonet blade (.12-inch thick) and aluminum handles. Users will appreci- ate its tip-up pocket clip and a lanyard hole. It measures 4.5 inches closed, 8 inches overall, and weighs 3.5 oz.

Other folders in the Schrade Alpha Class line include the Melee, Truix, and Radok, along with the Alkymest butterfly flipper.

In order to appeal to everyone's interests and purchasing ability, knife buyers will be delighted to find additional offerings in Schrade's new Beta and Delta lines.

Learn more about all Schrade products at their website: schrade.com ▲

Schrade Alpha Series introduced 2022: (top to bottom) Melee Auto, Truix, Radok, Alkemyst

CHAPTER 1

THE ESSENTIALS: HOW TO SOUND LIKE YOU KNOW WHAT YOU'RE TALKING ABOUT

The knife is an old tool. First, our ancestors hit with rocks that split into sharp shards. They learned to use these shards as cutting tools to make tasks easier. The rest is history as these cutting tools helped form the bedrock of civilization, making all sorts of human development possible. We eventually moved beyond simple rocks to finely crafted knapped tools, and then later to copper, bronze, and iron. Steel came later, and we now enjoy an age when there are literally hundreds of types of steel that can make knives that greatly outperform cutting tools from any other time in history.

With that in mind, let's break down the essential components of a modern knife and explore why each is important. Whether the knife is made in a factory by the hundreds or one at a time by a single craftsman, the principles in this chapter will apply. Chapter two dives in deeper to the specific terms and definitions, but for now we will stick with some broad principles.

Form Follows Function

At its simplest, a knife is a means to safely hold a cutting edge during use. Throughout the history of mankind, the form of a tool has often been based on the tool's intended function. Hammers are heavier on the head end than the handle end. Wheels are round so that they'll roll. A smith need only look to his collection of tongs to understand that the jaw types are useful for holding different sizes and styles of work pieces. For a working tool, the form of the tool should be suited to the job for which it is designed.

The first question a knife buyer should consider is, "what is this knife designed to do?" Knives can be made for peeling potatoes, carrying in the pocket, stabbing bad guys, skinning varmints, chopping jungle underbrush and many other tasks. Not surprisingly, a pen blade on a stockman folder is not the

---

When buying a knife with function in mind, one should consider what characteristics of the knife make it well suited to the intended job. A single knife has many design elements that fall under "form" that ultimately influence its functionality.

same shape and size as a kukri or a machete. When buying a knife with function in mind, one should consider what characteristics of the knife make it well suited to the intended job. A single knife has many design elements that fall under "form" that ultimately influence its functionality.

"Form follows function" is a foundational principle of using knives, but also carries over into art knives or knives collected for sentimental or other reasons, too. If you buy a knife as an investment and it goes up in value, then the form has followed the function. If you buy a piece of knife-shaped art and your significant other is impressed with your artistic vision, then form has followed function.

Thick Or Thin?

A knife blade may be ground or forged from stock that is thick or thin. In general, thick knives are more durable, have greater chopping power, feel heavier in the hand, and are often capable of more kinetic work like digging or prying. Thin knife blades are generally less durable, not likely to excel at clearing brush, but much more efficient at cutting and slicing. We all recognize that you could slice a tomato with a katana or skin a bear with a paring knife, but we also intuitively recognize that the knife should be suited to each particular task with regard to its thickness and cutting characteristics.

Ground Or Forged?

In times past and today, the argument over the relative merits of forging versus stock removal has been a rabbit trail to nowhere. Let's start with what these words mean. A knife is "forged" if it is manipulated to shape by the maker using heat. In simple terms, you get it hot and hit it with a hammer until it's in the shape of a knife.

A "stock removal" knife starts with a steel bar and then is shaped into a knife using abrasives. Simply, you grind off everything that isn't a knife. Given today's modern steel manufacturing techniques and the availability of quality heat treating equipment and information, I can confidently say that there is no functional difference in the end product between forged and stock removal knives.

Sure, some steels do better with one process or the other, and some makers take advantage of the different characteristics of the two processes, but in the end, the cutting performance of two equal knives will be identical regardless of whether the steel was forged or ground. In broad generality, carbon and tool steels work better with forging, and stainless steels are well suited for stock removal. Any differences in performance between equivalent properly hardened forged and stock removal knives will be the result of grind geometry and steel selection.

Even though the functionality is the same, some collectors may prefer forged knives because of

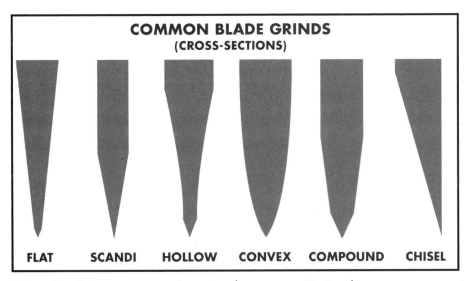

COMMON BLADE GRINDS
(CROSS-SECTIONS)

FLAT   SCANDI   HOLLOW   CONVEX   COMPOUND   CHISEL

Blade grinds you'll often come across can be seen here. (Image courtesy of Knafs.com)

the connection to historical skills or the appearance of primitivity. Others may prefer knives made from the latest and greatest super-steels (complex alloyed stainless steels) because of the superb performance or the appearance of modernity. We are free to prefer what we prefer when it comes to using or collecting, but let's not pretend that either forged or stock

removal is the universally best process. There is a chapter later that dives into the various steel types, their various attributes, and how to pick a steel based on what it can do for you.

Blade Grinds

Cutting performance is greatly influenced by the way in which the maker grinds the knife. Each grind will have different cutting characteristics. A good knifemaker will consider whether the grind of the knife is suited to the chosen task. You as a buyer will also need to consider if the grind of a knife will suit the tasks you have in mind.

Some knives are ground with a flat bevel. A flat-ground knife is a simple wedge and may be thick or thin. Flat grinds are good for slicing and deep cuts. I personally prefer a flat grind that goes all the way to the spine. A thinner flat grind will cut more smoothly than a thicker flat grind, where a thicker grind may be more durable.

A hollow-ground knife has a slightly concave bevel, which makes it thinner behind the cutting edge. This makes for good skinning and shallow cut work, with-out giving up overall blade heft or durability. Deep cuts or chopping are not well suited to a hollow grind.

Convex grinds have slightly rounded bevels, which increases their edge stability. While they may not excel at slicing, they're the way to go for hard use cutting and chopping.

Scandi grinds are a short flat grind with no secondary bevel. "Scandi" refers to the Scandinavian countries where that grind style is popular, espe-cially Finland. This grind style cuts very well but can be difficult to sharpen properly.

A compound grind may com-bine several of the basic grind shapes. Particularly on tactical and folding knives, many modern

STRAIGHT BACK
This standard shape is useful for piercing, skinning, and bushcraft. Scandinavian puukko knives typically feature this shape.

DROP POINT
The drop point is used on many hunting and EDC knives. The strong tip and wide belly excel in most processing and slicing tasks. Popularized by Bob Loveless.

TANTO
Tantos are prime for piercing and have a heritage rooted in Japanese Samurai swords. Many tantos serve as tactical knives, and they're also useful for fine detail work.

CLIP POINT
Named for the crescent "clip" out of the spine of the blade, clip points are thinner in the spine for better piercing and withdrawal.

BOWIE
A type of clip point, the Bowie is also a specific type of knife that is large, heavy, and famous for its role in the Alamo and that Crocodile Dundee scene: "That's not a knife."

SHEEPSFOOT
This blade style has a near-blunt tip to avoid puncturing. Useful for first responders and working among inflatables like river rafts.

WHARNCLIFFE
The wharncliffe style was originally for whitling and EDC tasks, but in recent years, many tactical knives have adapted the style.

CLEAVER
The classic kitchen and butcher knife shape has evolved into an EDC/work blade shape that looks schweet and sizes well.

---

grinds are aesthetically interesting, but at the occasional sacrifice of performance. If you're collecting for aesthetic reasons, however, these grinds could be all you ever wanted out of a knife.

A long, thin blade may be ideal for filleting fish, but useless for shucking oysters. A sword is not a suitable substitute for a skinner, nor a bowie for a barber's razor. The shape of the blade—whether drop point, trailing point, or clip—and the shape and length of the handle have an impact on the knife's performance.

All images courtesy of Knafs.com.

SPEAR POINT
A symmetrical shape creates a long cutting edge that also excels at piercing. The top edge of a spear point is not sharp.

DAGGER
The dagger is designed specifically for piercing and is often found on tactical knives. The top and bottom edges are both sharp.

HAWKSBILL
This shape originated as a mini sickle for agriculture and has spread as a karambit for tactical, self defense, and mall ninjas alike.

LEAF SHAPE
This shape comes with a strong tip and plenty of belly in the blade for slicing. The uniform shape makes sharpening easier.

RECURVE
Recurves feature an "S" shape in the blade for a longer overall cutting edge that is excellent for slicing. The drawback is trickier sharpening.

KUKRI
A Nepalese style used as a utilitarian tool for chopping, clearing and building. It is also the cutting weapon of choice for the Nepalese military.

PERSIAN
Also called a "trailing point" or "upswept" blade. Used for skinning and butchering. Plus: includes Lawrence of Arabia street cred.

MODIFIED
Don't know what to call that blade shape? When in doubt, call it a modified ___ . No further questions asked.

Blade Shapes

The size and shape of the blade should also be suited to the task. A long, thin blade may be ideal for filleting fish, but useless for shucking oysters. A sword is not a suitable substitute for a skinner, nor a bowie for a barber's razor. The shape of the blade—whether drop point, trailing point, or clip—and the shape and length of the handle have an impact on the knife's performance. In terms of actual use, many prefer a knife point that comes in below the spine for skinning or gutting work. Knives intended for chopping don't need much point at all, and so you'll often see spear points or even blunt squared points on heavy chopping knives.

Form And Function Are A Balance

As you consider each attribute of the knife you have in mind, consider first whether that particular attribute complements the knife's intended function. The design should have characteristics that lend themselves to the knife's assigned task. Is the edge thin enough for your cutting tasks? Is the edge thick enough for your kinetic tasks? Is the blade shape useful for what you want to do with the knife?

There is no "perfect" knife, as each attribute is balanced by another. Only you as a buyer can ultimately decide what tradeoffs and attributes you prefer. One advantage to purchasing in person is you can ask the salesperson or knifemaker directly. They may be able to help you navigate some of the design tradeoffs and guide you toward a knife that will suit you well.

How Knives Are Made

Learning how to make knives can be a lifelong pursuit, but a rudimentary understanding of the knife building process is helpful for buying. Here are the basic steps by which all knives are created regardless of whether they're one-off customs or mass production.

1. Obtain suitable steel.

2. Shape the steel to near the final shape, either by forging or removing material.

3. Harden the steel by heating it and then cooling it rapidly.

4. Draw back the hardness by tempering to improve performance.

5. Polish or otherwise finish your blade.

6. Install a handle.

Suitable Steel

Steel is a uniform mix of iron and carbon atoms, with other elements sometimes mixed in to provide specific characteristics. Each alloy element beyond simple iron changes the properties of the final product. Generally, hardenable knife steel typically contains between 0.6 and 1.5 percent carbon. There is a chapter later in this book that goes into some more detail regarding the various steel types.

Broadly speaking, there are two main categories you're likely to see in a knife: stainless steel and carbon steel. Stainless steel is generally more resistant to corrosion, while carbon steel lends itself better to forging and is easier to harden with simple equipment. While there are other steel types such as alloy steel or tool steel, for now the stainless/carbon categorization is enough.

In general, I find that it is often easier to sharpen carbon steel than stainless. On the other hand, stainless steels are preferred in harsh environments or kitchen scenarios. Within these broad categories, each maker will have their preferences. You'll develop preferences for steels you prefer and steels you avoid as your experience grows.

Another angle on this issue is to ask, "what steel is suitable?" That question is perhaps best answered by naming a few steels that are NOT suitable, and a few other steels that seem like they would work well but really do not.

Steel from the local big box hardware store is not suitable, as it does not contain enough carbon to harden properly. Railroad spikes are not suitable steel to make a high-performance knife. Even those spikes marked "HC" for "high carbon" only have around 0.3% carbon and will not make a knife that will hold an edge. Free things are fun, and much has been written about places to find knife steel among junk. Commonly mentioned are "old files." How do you know if a file is old, and how old is old enough? No one knows for sure.

"Lawnmower blades" are in the same category. While I am quite sure there have been suitable knives made out of lawnmower blades, and I know of at least one master smith who made lawnmower blades out of hardened O1 knife steel, most modern lawnmower blades are made overseas to minimum specifications by the lowest bidder. Do you want to start with the cheapest material the manufacturer could get by with? I don't.

Some folks will also recommend "leaf springs." I have personally made quality knives out of leaf spring material. I've also put time and effort into leaf spring knives only to have the steel fail miserably due to either unseen flaws or insufficient carbon content. Leaf spring knives take a level of experience to do well.

I will also say that there are reasons that knifemakers use found steel, but these reasons aren't related to cost. If you want to make a knife out of your grandfather's file, out of your customer's farm implement or out of a classic car's leaf spring, go for it. The cool factor sometimes makes unknown steel worth the risks involved.

Steel is among the cheapest parts of the knife. Consider that a four-foot bar of 1084 may cost $24, or $6 a foot. A three-foot bar of 154CM stainless may cost $60, or $20 a foot. Fine damascus steel may cost $20+ an *inch*. Even so, when made into an 8-inch blade, the steel cost is $4 in 1084, $13.33 in 154CM, and $160 in Damascus. Considering that out of my shop a standard 8-inch knife in 1084 might bring $300-$400 in carbon or stainless, my steel cost represents somewhere between 1% and 3% of the final price in standard steels. Even in high-priced damascus, my steel cost is at maximum around 25%.

The thing to remember is that when you purchase a knife made from unknown steel, or steel that is listed in a generic way, you have no assurance of quality beyond the skill of the maker, and no guarantee of performance. A label that simply says "stainless," or the German equivalent "Rostfrei," really doesn't tell you anything at all about the actual performance of the steel or its composition, except that it is less likely to rust. In the same way, if you're told by a maker or manufacturer that a knife is "carbon steel," don't take that for an answer. Ask "which one?"

Shaping The Blade

There are two basic approaches to taking steel from bar stock to a knife shape.

One way is to forge the steel. This involves heating the steel up in a fire—most often coal or propane—and hammering it into shape. This requires a heat source, some way to hold the work, a hammer, and something to hit against (like an anvil).

The other way to shape a knife is to buy bars of steel and grind or cut them to shape using abrasives or an endmill. Simply put, you grind or mill off everything that isn't a knife. Basic stock removal tools may include files, bench grinders, angle grinders, or belt grinders. More advanced tools include variable speed grinders, milling machines and CNC (computer numerically controlled) milling or grinding equipment.

A final factor that goes to shape not covered previously is the symmetry of the grind. On a fine knife, the transition from handle flats to the blade bevels, which is called the plunge cut, will be even and symmetrical. The edge will be centered, and the curves of the plunge will be the same on both sides.

Hardening

Steel is hard compared to wood or silly putty, but the knife steel that makers and manufacturers buy from their suppliers is soft relative to its final state. In order to make raw knife steel into a performing knife, it must be hardened. The basic hardening process requires heating steel to its "critical temperature." The critical temperature of steel is determined by its carbon content and its alloy content, and may also include a "soak" time in order for the knife to harden properly.

Once the steel has reached critical temperature and soaked the right amount of time, it is quickly cooled. This is called "quenching" the steel. Some steels quench simply by cooling in air. These are called "air hardening" steels. They also can be hardened by placing them between aluminum plates in a process called "plate quench-ing." Other steels quench in oil. The type of oil must be suited to the composition of the steel.

Some people confuse the terms "heat treating," "harden-ing" and "tempering." In my mind, heat treating is the entire process of taking a knife from raw stock to finished blade. Heat treating includes both hardening and tempering, as well as optional steps such as normalizing, an-nealing, thermal cycling or cryo-genic cooling.

Hardening is the process I de-scribed above, bringing the steel to critical and then cooling it quickly. Tempering is the process by which your hardened steel knife is made less brittle, so that your edge will perform well. While hardening may require special equipment and temperatures between 1,500-and 2,000-degrees Fahrenheit, tempering can often be completed in your kitchen oven's temperature range.

Another consideration is the final hardness of the knife. In general, a quality knife will have a Rockwell C hardness of 58 to 61. There will be exceptions, and you should choose the final hard-ness of your knife based on how you want it to perform. Knives on the softer end of the range will sharpen more easily. Knives on the harder end of the range will hold an edge longer but will be more likely to chip. There is further information about the tradeoffs involved in heat treating in the later chapter on knife steel.

Finishing Work

A blade straight out of the heat treating process will require some finish work. This most commonly involves using abrasives of increasingly finer grit to remove metal until the blade reaches the level of smoothness that the manufacturer or maker requires. A typical, user-grade knife is finished to at least 400 grit, while many fine knives are hand finished to 1,500 grit, or are machine polished to a mirror finish. The higher the grit number, the finer the finish.

There are several keys to a clean, uniform finish on a knife blade. A clean finish starts with a good, clean grind. Whether flat or hollow, a quality knife's primary grind should have no bobbles, dips, wiggles, or anything else other than a clean grind at the chosen finish grit.

The knife's final finish should be uniform, with no underlying heavier grit grind marks. The final finish should also be in one direction (i.e.

Remember this: "Thin is in, and light is right." On the other hand, some people with conditions like arthritis or carpal tunnel may prefer a fatter handle. If it feels right in your hand, it's right.

spine to bevel or plunge to tip) but not both on the same knife.

Can You Handle It?

When it comes to handle design, consider again how form follows function. Is the size of the handle suitable to the task at hand, and suitable to the blade you've constructed? Any sharp corners on the handle will impact your experience in negative ways.

There should be no sharp corners on a custom knife's handle. The handle should be at least oval or egg shaped in profile, not a square with rounded corners. This happens because the knifemaker is scared to remove too much material. Remember this: "Thin is in, and light is right." On the other hand, some people with conditions like arthritis or carpal tunnel may prefer a fatter handle. If it feels right in *your* hand, it's right.

Handles are typically fastened with glue and mechanical fasteners. Modern, two-part epoxy is the glue of choice. Epoxy joints have good strength perpendicular to the joint, but tend to be weaker when sheared across the joint. Therefore, the vast majority of knives will include pins in the handle material to increase the shear strength of the handle-to-blade junction. Others prefer the belt-and-suspenders approach and use a true mechanical fastener such as a Corby, Loveless bolt or threaded pommel in addition to the glue joint.

The handle material you choose should also be suited to the knife's intended purpose. The basic categories are wood, synthetic, and animal products such as bone, horn or ivory. Each has its place in the knife world.

Wood is natural, and can be either plain or beautiful. It can also be tough and durable like hickory or ash, or fragile like unstabilized burl. Some woods are stabilized by using pressure to saturate the wood with a polymer resin. Other woods are dense or oily enough that they don't benefit from stabilization.

Bone, horn and antler have been used as knife handles for centuries. They tend toward durability, but may also crack with age. You are also somewhat limited by the natural shapes available.

Ivory is a material that deserves more discussion, as the ins and outs are complicated. Ivory comes from several sources and may be "good" or "bad" depending on the source and the rules of your particular state or jurisdiction.

In general, "fossil" ivory comes from the tusks of walrus or mammoth specimens long dead or even completely extinct. This ivory has been in the ground or the sea for literally thousands of years. Using fossil ivory doesn't kill an animal and has no impact on the current population of any of the world's favorite beasts.

"Modern" ivory comes primarily from elephants killed in the last couple hundred years. There are various bans on ivory importation and trading, and each state may have its own rules as well. Be sure that nobody in the knife world controls or influences the ivory market, but the whims of animal lovers and governments certainly influence the use of ivory by knifemakers.

In my personal opinion, the use of fossil ivory should be universally allowed, and the use of modern ivory harvested legally should also be categorically allowed. You'll have to form your own opinion about whether ivory is right for you.

In terms of material properties, fossil ivory is old enough to be fairly stable. It doesn't tend to crack, and swells or contracts very little with changes in humidity or temperature. Modern ivory is more prone to cracking and movement.

Also, consider whether the handle material is prone to cracking or discoloration, whether the blade will rust or tarnish, and whether the fitting material is likely to change color over time. None of these are necessarily a deal breaker, but when you buy a knife for your collection you should have reasonable expectations for what kind of maintenance it may require.

The Dishwasher Rule

Regardless of what you choose, don't *ever* put your knife in the dishwasher. The knife gods will most certainly smite thee.

It's Simple, But It Isn't

In the end, the process sounds simple. The truth is that there are steps within the steps, and details within the details. As you progress in your knowledge, you'll learn to spot smaller and smaller mistakes, and decide which ones you can live with and which ones you can't. You'll think of questions you never thought of, and then you'll find the answers. You'll develop preferences on what kinds of materials, shapes, and designs that you like best.

Every collector has something to learn, no matter what they've accomplished, and every collector has something to teach, no matter how long they've been on the journey. This introductory overview is simply introductory.

Dive into the advanced material in the chapters to come. Read on, my friend! ▲

CHAPTER 2

ALL THE KNIFE TERMS YOU NEED TO KNOW

Every niche has its own lingo. Part of learning a new subject is to learn the words that people use when they discuss that subject. Fortunately for us, the language of the knife world isn't as complex as the technical words folks in medical or engineering use.

In this chapter, I'll break down the knife jargon into plain English, so that we can all know a "ricasso" or "detent" when we see one.

I'm going to give you folks some credit for knowing how to read, and not going to dive in hard on all these words when the knife use matches the common use of a word. A handle is a handle, the thing you put your hand on, for example.

Let's start with a fixed blade.

Basic Parts Of A Fixed Blade Knife

A knife **guard** is the piece in between the handle and the blade, that "guards" your hand from sliding up to the cutting edge. A guard can be below the handle or can be a "double guard" and extend both above and below the handle like the one on the diagram.

The **ricasso** of a knife is the flat un-sharpened spot between the handle and the plunge. They come

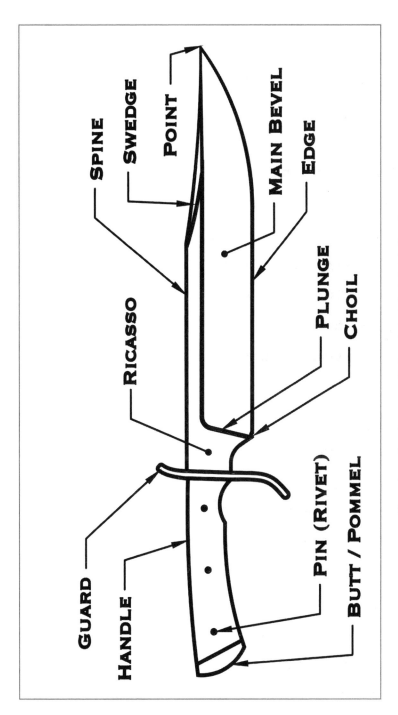

The parts—and words—you need to know to go graduate from knife noob.

in all shapes and sizes, but you'll notice later that even a folding knife or a sword can have a ricasso. Ricasso size and proportion are somewhat subjective, but the "golden ratio" is a good place to start. A "golden ratio" ricasso will be about 1.6 times deeper than it is wide. A 1-inch-tall ricasso at the golden ratio is about 0.6 inches wide.

The **spine** of a knife is the top of the blade, while the **edge** is the bottom of the blade.

The **swedge** is a beveled area on the spine. A swedge can be "cut" where there's a plunge along the spine where the swedge starts, or "drawn" where the swedge fades into the spine as in the example picture. Swedges can be sharpened all the way to a cutting edge. A sharpened swedge is also sometimes called a "clip," even though in my mind a clip is more of a profile geometry. An unsharpened swedge can also be called a "false edge."

The **bevel** of a knife is the area where the blade transitions from spine thickness to edge thickness. There are quite a few variations in how this transition is shaped, and each has its own name. These are described elsewhere in this book. Sometimes the "main bevel" is distinguished from the "secondary bevel" or "sharpening bevel," the area where the main bevel transitions into the actual cutting edge.

Choil is a word that's used to describe several different things, all of which have to do with the transition area between the ricasso and edge. In the first picture, the choil is the point of the back of the sharpened edge. In the second picture, the choil is the little half-round cutout in between the edge and the ricasso. Sometimes this style is called a "sharpening choil." If the choil is enlarged so you can grip the knife there, it may be called a "finger choil." A "Spanish notch" is a decorative kind of choil seen on fixed blades.

The transition between the ricasso and the main bevel is called the **plunge**. Plunges can be swooping or squared, gradual or dramatic, so long as they are symmetrical on both sides of the knife. Some knives have a "faded plunge" where the transition is gradual so that there is no obvious corner between the ricasso and bevel.

Handle fasteners come in many shapes and sizes and go by many names. Sometimes, as in the first picture, they're simple "pins," pieces of metal stuck through the handle. Other times they're "rivets," a two-piece assembly hammered together. Other times, regular screws are used to fasten the handle in a variety of ways. There are even specialized screw designs like "Corbys" and "Loveless bolts." They all serve the same purpose, which is to secure the handle to the tang of the knife.

A knife **tang** is the part of the blade that extends into the handle. A "full tang" knife has the blade steel visible all the way around the handle, with the handle material fastened to the side of the knife. Various shapes and configurations of "hidden tang" knives have the metal inset or stuck in a hole within the handle itself. This is illustrated in the graphic on page 35 with the fixed blade knife.

The end of the handle of the knife is called the **butt**. If the butt has a cover, it can be called either a "butt cap" or a "pommel." I tend to only use pommel if the entire piece is threaded or pinned on to the tang, as on a vintage Kabar, for example.

Basic Parts Of A Folding Knife

Many of the same elements from the fixed blade knife carry over into the folding knife, with similar or identical definitions. The spine, edge, choil, ricasso, bevel, swedge and point are all the same.

This graphic also includes a **flat**, the area of full thickness steel between the bevel and the spine.

A **thumb stud** is a feature used to open and close the knife with your thumb. Other options for this feature and function are a hole, a disk, a dual thumb stud, or several other patented designs.

Jimping is the addition of grooves along the spine of the knife to aid in grip. This feature is common on both fixed blade and folding knives. Occasionally, there will be jimping along a finger choil or on the point of the flipper as well.

This folding knife has a **lanyard hole**—literally a hole where you can attach a lanyard. It's also sometimes called a "thong hole" and can be found on fixed blades as well.

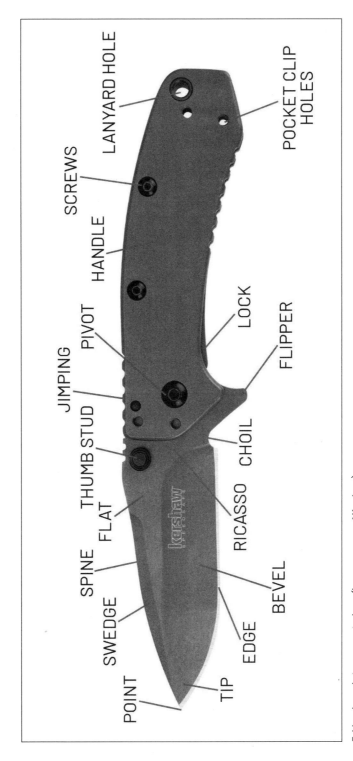

Folders have their own terminology. (Image courtesy of Kershaw.)

The lock is the mechanism by which a folding knife is held open.

The knife has a **flipper**. It's not a flipper like a dolphin or a seal or scuba diver. It's a protrusion by which the blade is opened with a flip. There are also "front flippers" where the knife flips open from a protrusion on the front, compared to a regular flipper that's on the side of the closed knife.

In the center of the knife is the **pivot**, or the point at which the blade turns within the handle. There are many pivot designs, including everything from a pinned slipjoint pivot up through complex machined pivot mechanisms on automatics and high-end folders like the Ron Appleton in the color section.

Types Of Knives

While I personally like the types of knives classified by basic design, there are other ways to classify knives by type. Another way is to think about knives grouped in terms of function or intended use (see graphic on page 36).

Within each category, there are other distinctions. The graphic on page 37 shows several different types of folding knife locks.

And if you break it down further still, sometimes each subcategory has specific distinctions. There are quite a few different types of slipjoint folding knives shown on page 38.

Ways To Describe Blade Finish

Each blade finish has a name,

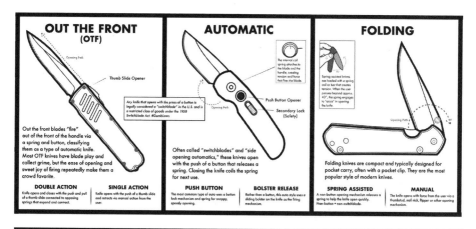

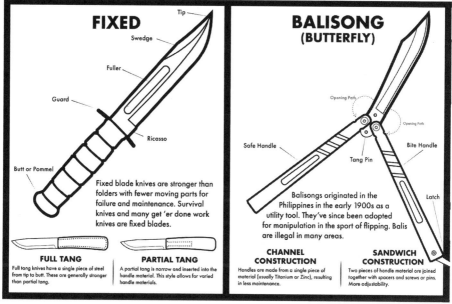

Images courtesy of Knafs.com.

and while they're fairly intuitive, it's handy to know what they're called so that you don't embarrass yourself by asking to see the "kinda shiny" one.

On a **satin finish**, you'll see fine brush, grind or sanding marks. In general, a machine satin finish will have these marks running from spine to edge, where a hand-sand-

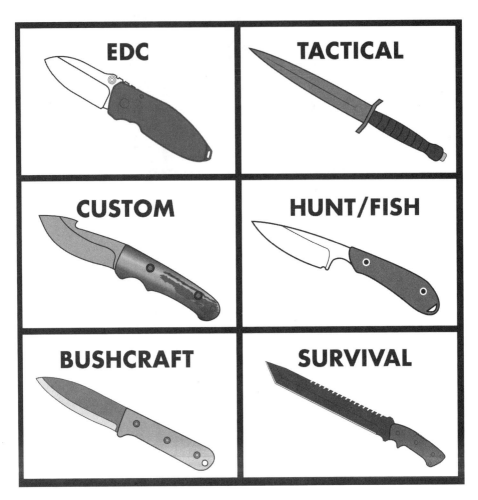

EDC

TACTICAL

CUSTOM

HUNT/FISH

BUSHCRAFT

SURVIVAL

Images courtesy of Knafs.com.

ed satin finish will run the length of the blade. You may see finish grits anywhere from 220 on up to 2,000 called a satin finish, but don't let that guy with 36 grit scratches fool you with his "satin."

A **stonewash** finish is applied using a vibratory or rotary tumbler and a polishing media. Sometimes the stonewash media is actual

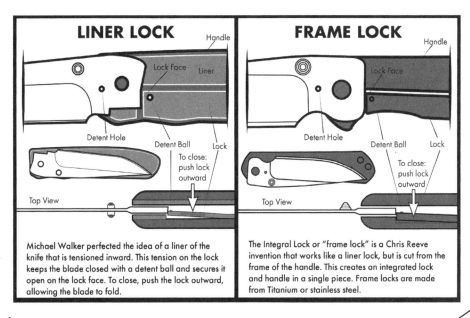

LINER LOCK

Handle
Lock Face
Liner
Detent Hole
Detent Ball
Lock
To close:
push lock
outward
Top View

Michael Walker perfected the idea of a liner of the knife that is tensioned inward. This tension on the lock keeps the blade closed with a detent ball and secures it open on the lock face. To close, push the lock outward, allowing the blade to fold.

FRAME LOCK

Handle
Lock Face
Detent Hole
Detent Ball
Lock
To close:
push lock
outward
Top View

The Integral Lock or "frame lock" is a Chris Reeve invention that works like a liner lock, but is cut from the frame of the handle. This creates an integrated lock and handle in a single piece. Frame locks are made from Titanium or stainless steel.

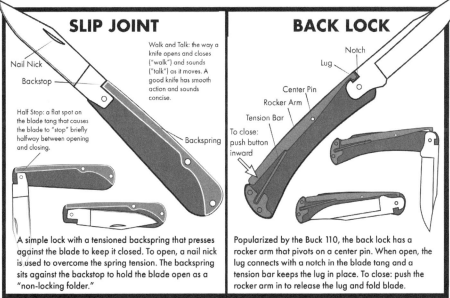

SLIP JOINT

Nail Nick
Backstop
Half Stop: a flat spot on the blade tang that causes the blade to "stop" briefly halfway between opening and closing.

Walk and Talk: the way a knife opens and closes ("walk") and sounds ("talk") as it moves. A good knife has smooth action and sounds concise.

Backspring

A simple lock with a tensioned backspring that presses against the blade to keep it closed. To open, a nail nick is used to overcome the spring tension. The backspring sits against the backstop to hold the blade open as a "non-locking folder."

BACK LOCK

Notch
Lug
Center Pin
Rocker Arm
Tension Bar
To close:
push button
inward

Popularized by the Buck 110, the back lock has a rocker arm that pivots on a center pin. When open, the lug connects with a notch in the blade tang and a tension bar keeps the lug in place. To close: push the rocker arm in to release the lug and fold blade.

Images courtesy of Knafs.com.

COMMON TRADITIONAL KNIFE PATTERNS

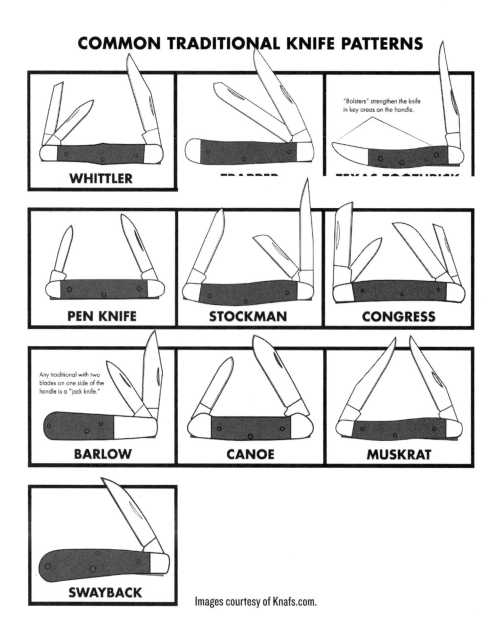

"Bolsters" strengthen the knife in key areas on the handle.

WHITTLER

TRAPPER

TEXAS TOOTHPICK

PEN KNIFE

STOCKMAN

CONGRESS

Any traditional with two blades on one side of the handle is a "jack knife."

BARLOW

CANOE

MUSKRAT

SWAYBACK

Images courtesy of Knafs.com.

stones or ceramic stones, and sometimes it's other things, but they're all usually just called stonewashed or "tumbled."

A **beadblast** finish is blasted with beads. Who would have thought! They can be glass beads, ceramic beads, steel beads (shot

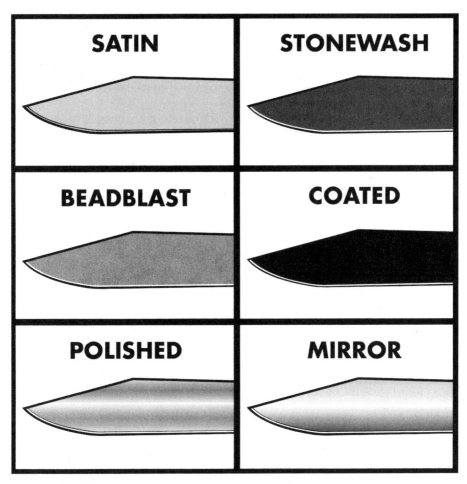

Images courtesy of Knafs.com.

blasting) or even sand (sandblasting). The finish for each blasting media will be slightly different, but they all create a blasted finish. In this kind of blasting, they use compressed air and a thin nozzle.

Don't get all excited thinking about dynamite.

There are several kinds of **coated** finishes. A common one is called Cerakote, a proprietary ceramic coating process. Powder coating uses powder. These words mean what they say: a coating of something else is applied on top of the blade steel.

A **polished** finish in my mind is a fine satin finish that's not full mirror. This is a pretty fine distinction in my mind, as polishing is a broad process.

A **mirror** finish is the only one OK to call "the shiny one." A mirror finish should resemble a mirror. Go figure. You'll see a mirror finish in two places, for two different reasons. On one end, you'll see a mirror finish with washed out edges on amateur or production knives. You can get a shiny finish by buffing with aggressive rouge, but it makes for no crisp lines. At the high end you'll see a mirror finish that truly shines with no underlying scratches or bobbles, and with crisp grind lines. It takes practice, skill, and good equipment to get a high-quality mirror finish.

Knife Origin Categories

It is important that the maker or manufacturer of a knife honestly disclose how that knife came to be. Is it somehow wrong to manufacture a knife in China? Not if it says "Made in China" on it. Is it wrong to buy a bunch of Chinese parts, assemble them in Rhode Island, and stamp the knife "Made in USA?" In my mind, that's a bit dishonest, but the law allows it.

My beef is not with any knife in any of these categories, but rather with the makers or companies who intentionally misrepresent or obscure their knives' origin. To be clear, these definitions I'm about to put forth are often as much gray as they are black and white.

A **production knife** is any knife that was made in a factory by a company. Some factories include mostly machines, CNC equipment and so forth, while other companies rely more on hand work. This is not necessarily a "bad" or less valuable category. Buck, Benchmade, Schrade, Kershaw, Case and countless other reputable American companies fit this category.

At the other end of the spectrum is the **custom knife**. This knife is made one at a time by a specific maker. Think "bespoke" or "commissioned" for the purest use of this term. Some will argue it's not "custom" if it's not made specifically to a buyer's unique

Is it somehow wrong to manufacture a knife in China? Not if it says "Made in China" on it. Is it wrong to buy a bunch of Chinese parts, assemble them in Rhode Island, and stamp the knife "Made in USA?" In my mind, that's a bit dishonest, but the law allows it.

specifications, but I think that's splitting frog hairs. If it's made one at a time by a single craftsman, I'm OK calling it "custom."

Even within the custom knife world, there are debates about whether a knife is "handmade" or not. The Knifemakers' Guild, one of the professional knifemaking organizations, considers a knife handmade if the maker personally grinds and polishes the bevels and installs the handle. There are also purists who take pride in doing 100 percent of the work on knife, defined as every part that takes the maker's skill. Beyond that are the true fanatics who even make their own screws.

Another term you'll hear is **sole authorship**. For a knife to be considered sole authorship, all elements must be the work of a single maker. If someone else does the engraving, makes the damascus bar stock, or does the heat treating, in my mind the knifemaker shouldn't claim that knife is sole authorship.

I've saved for last the fuzziest

... if a factory makes a limited run of a special design to a maker's specifications, that's a hair past the line out of "midtech" and into production.

category of all: "midtech." A **midtech knife** is made by combining elements of production and custom/handmade work methods. In my mind, the guy who buys parts, has his blades ground, and then puts the knives together is definitely midtech. The guy who has his blades waterjet cut and then sends batches out for heat treat but then does all the grind and finish work, I'd say that's not midtech.

There's an invisible line where the machines or the production processes take a bit away from the hand work, and "midtechs" are right past that line. At the same time, if a factory makes a limited run of a special design to a maker's specifications, that's a hair past the line out of "midtech" and into production.

Within the category of full disclosure being important are the folks who put a handle on a knife blank made by someone else. In this case, a **knife blank** is a manufactured knife made for cutlers to install handles or fittings. As before, I have no problem with a guy putting handles on a set of steak knives, but he crosses the line if he says he "made" them. There are plenty of people in the knife world who will tell you that they "made" a knife when really they bought a ground, hardened, and polished blank from a store and put a handle on it. That's misrepresentation.

Random Terms

Micarta® is a Norplex-trademarked, laminate product

of phenolic resin plus a reinforcing material. The most common varieties are paper, linen and canvas. Although only Norplex Micarta can be called "micarta," the term is used generically in the knife world, like how all tissues are "Kleenex." Pretty much every paper, linen or canvas laminate is called "micarta." This trademark was previously owned by Westinghouse, and so true Westinghouse product can be rightly called Micarta.

G10 is a laminate product that features fiberglass layers in resin. Besides being fairly indestructible, another great feature is that it's available in some super crazy and bright colors.

The nail nick is the little cutout on a folding knife blade that allows the user to open the blade with a fingernail. It's common on slipjoints and lockbacks.

A fuller is a groove that runs down the blade between the edge and the spine. Some people call it a "blood groove" or "blood fuller," but those people are a little dramatic. The fuller's primary function is to reduce weight or adjust balance, with a secondary function of adding to the aesthetics of the knife.

Quillons are the points of a guard on a dagger. You'll rarely see this word anywhere but in the discussion of daggers. ▲

Credit: Graphics by Ben Petersen. Used with Permission. Copyright 2018. Available as a printed poster, Knives: A Modern Guide to Our Oldest Tool, *on Knafs.com.*

CHAPTER 3

ONLINE KNIFE PHOTOS
DON'T TELL THE WHOLE STORY

I'll let you in on some knife secrets. Do you know how easy it is to make an online picture look better than the real thing? Do you think selective picture editing never happens in the knife world? The wise knife buyer knows these things happen and takes them into account.

There are a few ways to make a knife look better than it might be in real life. One, depending on the angle of the shot, the blade-to-handle ratio changes.

Two, some angles show the best parts of a knife and obscure the worst parts. The standard side-on shot often used by makers and dealers is very helpful for deciding if you like the profile, if you like the blade-to-handle ratio, if you prefer the handle material or the look of the blade finish. That same shot also doesn't show you anything about whether the plunges are even, the blade is straight or whether the tip is centered on a folding knife. Depending on the angle, you may not be able to see the guard fitup or whether the bolsters are fitted evenly. This is not to suggest that a quality outfit will manipulate the angles to hide flaws, but not all outfits have the same values.

Examine these two pictures from the author. Neither is set up to conceal flaws, but the side profile shot doesn't let you check out the bolster fit, handle fit or tang taper. The spine shot doesn't give you any information about the plunge, the blade shape or the blade finish. Each shot angle only reveals a portion of the critical elements.

Inspect What You Expect

The moral is to "inspect what you expect," especially when so many knives are purchased online. If you have high standards or are paying a high price, you owe it to yourself to do your due diligence and examine those pictures and knives carefully. Alternatively, if you don't like what you see in the pictures, the odds are pretty good the knife will be worse in person.

Choose carefully, because once you've paid the money for a knife, you've made your choice. Two days or two weeks later after you've made the purchase, you shouldn't send it back. While the maker or dealer has a responsibility to represent the knife accurately, and the buyer may have a legitimate case to make an issue of a misrepresented knife, buying on the internet is a "buyer beware" scenario.

That's why understanding the concept of "fit and finish" is so important *before* you put down money for a knife, whether in-person or online. The following applies to both custom and factory knives, and everything that falls between.

"Fit And Finish?"

"Fit and finish" is the degree to which the elements of a knife are clean and tight. Fit and finish often varies with price. You may expect a few errors on a $100 knife that would be unacceptable on a $300 knife. Once you get to the mid level, around $500 to $1,500, the knives had better be darn good, and any errors had better be small

In this picture, notice the gaps between the bolster and the blade. Other errors include asymmetrical shaping, pins of a different material than the bolster, and an edge that is too thick prior to sharpening. Maker's mark is digitally obscured.

or well hidden. At the high end, there is an expectation that there will be very few points of error, or none at all.

There are many elements of a knife that must fit together tightly. A quality knife should not have any gaps on the handle between the scales and tang. There should not be any gaps or lines between the handle material and bolsters or guard. There should be no gap between the tang of a knife and pinned bolsters, and a tight fit between the guard slot and ricasso of a stick tang knife. Black glue can hide some minor gaps on dark material, whereas wide gaps are a major error even when filled with glue.

As a knife's complexity increases, so does the opportunity for fit error. A full tang knife may have as few as two joints—those between each handle side and the tang. On the other hand, a frame-handled bowie or fine folding knife may have a dozen or more points that must be fit up tightly without gaps.

Folding knives have a few other areas of fit that are critical. The blade should be centered evenly between the liners. The various elements along the back of the knife (liners, spring, back spacer, etc.) should be flush and uniformly fit.

Next for consideration is the quality of the knife's finish. There are several key points. One, the finish of the blade, handle, and fittings needs to be uniform. Whether the knife is "forge finished" or mirror polished, and

Karl Andersen demonstrates a well-finished plunge here. Note that all of the finish marks are in the same direction, with no underlying scratches. (Image courtesy of Andersen Forge)

whether the handle is Micarta or ivory, the finish of each element needs to be consistent, with no underlying scratches. The pattern of scratches should be clean and uniform. In my opinion, a knife blade can be called "finished" at a minimum of 400 grit, but I know others who would disagree in both the coarser and finer directions. Only the maker and buyer can decide if the finish is acceptable, but regardless of the final grit, there should be no unintentional marks.

I mentioned the finish of the handle material. Some materials like stag are best left with their natural texture, with just a few parts ground away and finished cleanly. Other materials like canvas Micarta or horse mat are good at "hiding" underlying scratches, and you can get away with a uniform 220- or even 120-grit finish on occasion.

Ivory and bone are some of the hardest to finish, as any underlying scratch is going to stand out very

> Common places to inspect for underlying scratches on the blade include the spine—particularly in the top middle of the knife—the low points of any finger grooves and the blade finish right up against the plunge cuts.

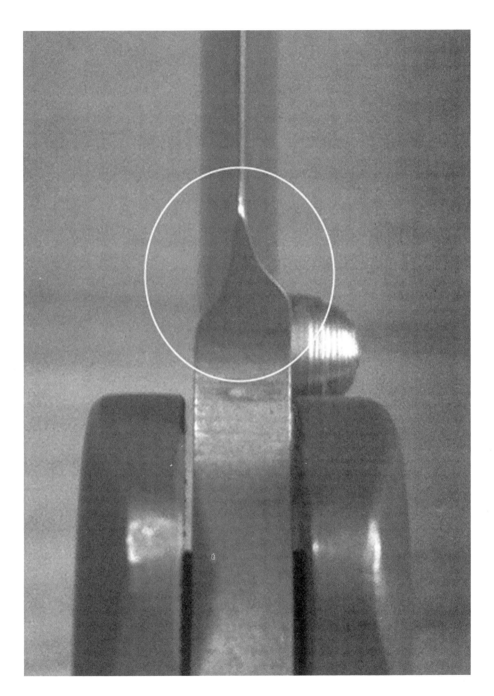

This is an example of a bag plunge. The symmetry is off.

badly. Areas to look for underlying handle scratches are inside any low spots like palm swells or finger grooves, and on the sides right at the butt between the back pin and the back edge of the handle.

Common places to inspect for underlying scratches on the blade include the spine—particularly in the top middle of the knife—the low points of any finger grooves and the blade finish right up against the plunge cuts. These are among the hardest areas to finish cleanly.

Symmetry

Symmetry also falls under the label of fit and finish. The shape of the finished knife should be symmetrical, particularly side to side. Handle shaping should result in a uniform oval or upside-down, egg-shaped profile at the butt, with no variation in shape or thickness on one side or the other. Any guard or bolsters should be evenly fit and symmetrically shaped. If it's different but not obviously intentional, it's not right. Sometimes even if it's intentional, it's still not right, but design and proportion are discussions for another day.

The plunges of a knife are an area where symmetry is critical. Whether the plunge cuts are square, rounded or even slowly swooped isn't relevant here, so long as the edge is centered, and the plunges are the same on both sides. When a discerning customer picks up a knife off my table and immediately checks the plunges, I know they're the real deal.

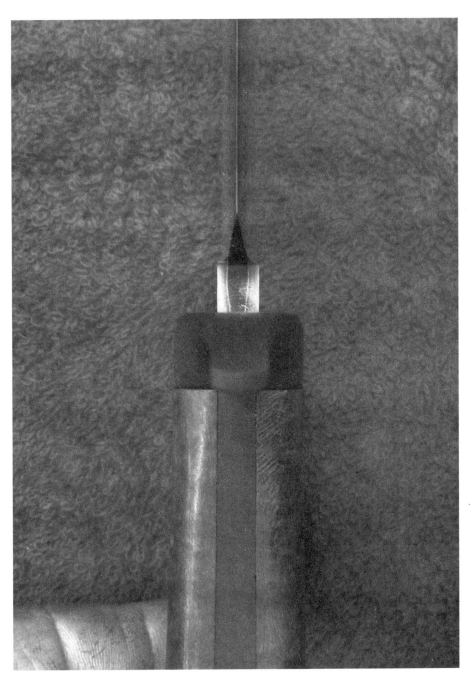

How about this one? Do you see symmetry in the plunge here? (Image courtesy of Andersen Forge)

The plunges should also terminate at the same height and angle at the top of the blade. This is an area that takes skill and effort to get right. This is also an area where the range of what's acceptable varies with price, but if the price is high, the plunges better be "dead nuts" correct.

Checking The Grind

The main bevel grind also merits further discussion. Any dips, bobbles or bumpy areas in the grind are errors, even if they're polished out to a uniform finish. A flat grind should be FLAT. A hollow grind should be evenly ground across the length of the blade.

One common place to find grind errors is 2 inches in front of the plunge. Sometimes the maker concentrates so much on getting the plunges right that the other edge of the grinding belt digs in a little. This 2-inch divot can appear on both flat and hollow ground knives.

Another factor of the blade grind is the edge geometry. The final edge geometry should be suited to the intended use of the knife. A thick convex grind may be perfect for an axe or even machete. A nearly invisible secondary bevel and a super-thin edge is desirable on a kitchen knife. Hunting knives should be somewhere between the two extremes.

One way to visibly check the edge thickness is to look at how wide the sharpening bevel is. If the bevel is wide, the grind may be too thick. If the bevel is very narrow, the edge is thin and the knife may fail if the heat treat wasn't just right.

Folding Knife Actions

Folding knives have another critical point to examine: the "action." Whether slipjoint or locking blade, the knife should open and close smoothly, with no gritty feeling or sticky spots. A slipjoint should "walk and talk," which means to open and close smoothly with a discernable snap at opening and closing positions and half stop. On a liner lock knife, the detent should be clean feeling, and the lock should not stick.

With that in mind, the "right" action for a folding knife can be up to personal preference.

Sharpness

I am of the strong opinion that a custom knife should come at least sharp enough to shave hair along the entire edge. While there are sharpness tests more discerning

---

I am of the strong opinion that a custom knife should come at least sharp enough to shave hair along the entire edge. While there are sharpness tests more discerning than arm hairs, cutting hair is a good place to start.

than arm hairs, cutting hair is a good place to start.

Occasionally a maker may miss this detail, but remember that we're talking about knives here. A dull knife isn't much of a knife at all. At the same time, a factory knife that comes duller than you want it should be considered an annoyance. Get out your preferred sharpening system, not your phone to call and complain, unless the company touts their sharpness or the knife is expensive. If you've purchased a midtech from the maker, I'd expect it to be sharp at the custom level. On the other hand, if you purchase it from a distributor, you may find that a less-sharp edge is acceptable.

Knowing How To Spot Errors Makes You A Better Buyer

In summary, there are many points of error possible on a knife, both custom and factory. Knife photos are a good place to start, but they don't tell the whole story. The discerning collector should strive to spot as many errors as possible and realize that no knife is 100-percent error free.

Only the maker can decide when a knife is "done" to the point where the mistakes are within the margin of error for the intended function and price point, and only the buyer can decide if those errors are "too much to live with" for the price they are going to pay.

The important thing is to "inspect what you expect" and make a solid informed buying decision. ▲

CHAPTER 4

HOW TO NOT GET RIPPED OFF WHEN BUYING CUSTOM KNIVES

'm not sure what would happen if one day I woke up and everything and everyone in the world was honest, straightforward and accurately represented. I'd think I had been abducted by aliens, because the world I'm familiar with is often deceptive, or at least has yucky consequences for my bad choices.

This chapter is about buying and selling collectible and custom knives. I'd love to say, "It's all good, just go buy one. Maybe buy a dozen, because it always works out great!" But we instinctively know that it's not "all good" all the time.

There are quite a few pitfalls to be aware of as you enter the knife buying world. This chapter will keep you out of a few of the pits, help you skirt the landmines and ultimately help you have a better buying experience with fewer regrets. I want to believe the best about people, so I'll save the warnings about "bad guys" until the end.

Basic Principles Of Knife Transactions

First off, let's think about a few free market principles. One, you tend to get what you pay for. The odds are pretty good that if a knife is being sold cheaply, it's cheap for a reason. If the price is high, there's usually a reason for that as well.

Sometimes supply and demand come in to play. If "everyone" wants a particular knife, but there are a limited number of them available, the basic laws of economics suggest that the price is going to go up.

As a good example, Bob Loveless died in 2010. That means that any demand cannot be moderated by increased supply, and so prices tend to move upward over time. On the flip side, if a maker finds a way to increase production, there's a chance that increased supply may push the price or desirability down a bit.

Another principle is that a deal isn't "bad" if it's mutually agreeable. If you agree to pay an asking price, and they deliver the product when you pay, then that's a "good" deal.

An old dickering buddy of mine used to say that a good deal is one where both parties feel like they "took" the other guy just a little bit. Your goal is to pay as little as

---

... you tend to get what you pay for. The odds are pretty good that if a knife is being sold cheaply, it's cheap for a reason. If the price is high, there's usually a reason for that as well.

possible, and their goal is for you to pay as much as possible, but if you agree on the price, a deal's a good deal.

Exceptions

Of course, every rule or principle has its exceptions and counter-principles. You do get what you pay for, but only when you have an honest and informed assessment. Is that micarta real Westinghouse *Micarta*? Is the fit and finish and reputation of the maker in line with the price? Did the maker grind the knife themselves, or is this a production knife?

You'll have to do some homework if you want to get "good deals." One of the oldest tricks in the book is for the seller to exaggerate demand and conceal supply. "This is the last one, and they've been buying them fast all day!" may be true or may be a dishonest sales pitch.

The warning is "buyer beware" more often than "seller beware" after all. Many a "bad deal" comes not from mutual disagreement, but from one side taking advantage or being dishonest.

Economic generalities aside, let's look specifically at the knife market.

Lesson 1:
Don't Buy The Hype

Some people want the latest and greatest thing. They get great enjoyment out of buying what is the ultimate "grail" knife of a given season, often hyped up on social media, on online forums, by word of mouth, in magazines and at events. For these buyers, the thrill is in the hunt and in the showing of the trophy.

If you want to be that kind of buyer, buy what you want and enjoy the heck out of it! Keep in mind that demand will be lower for last year's hot thing, and so will the resale price. I won't go so far as to say don't buy the hot knife. Many of us spend money on experiences (what do you gain long term from a concert or a trip to the movies?) or on depreciating possessions like cars or boats. In some ways, if you enjoy it, it doesn't matter if you lose some money on a knife or it's not a good "investment."

Many of us "regular" folks have to be a little more careful with our funds. If you chase what's hot,

> If you chase what's hot, you'll end up buying at times of peak demand, which means you'll pay a higher price.

you'll end up buying at times of peak demand, which means you'll pay a higher price. By the time you get tired of that knife or want to sell, everyone else just might be tired of it as well, as the knife world will have moved on to the next hot thing. If you're one of the folks for whom a sour ending ruins the whole experience, don't buy hot. If you have an eye toward appreciation of values and want to "make money" on your knife collecting hobby, don't buy hot.

For some people, the thrill is in finding the next hot one, before it gets hot. Wouldn't we all have loved to have purchased a bunch of Microsoft stock in 1993? If we were better at predicting the future, we'd make better knife picks for our collection, just like we'd make better choices in our stock portfolio. Still, if you "hit" one once in a while—buy the maker's work right before he hits the big time and make lots of money—it can be quite a thrill and keep you buying knives on a regular basis.

Another point of caution when it comes to hype has to do with the "flash in the pan" types who grow smoking hot quickly, beyond their market position or ability to produce. It has happened in the knife world before and will happen again. Someone may be better at marketing than knifemaking, or better at Instagram videos than filling knife orders. If the hype of a particular maker turns you off or looks suspicious, trust your gut and hold off on purchasing. Sometimes makers flame out as spectacularly as they rose to fame.

Lesson 2: Don't Overspend At The Beginning

"Walk before you run" is good advice. Knife collecting is about finding joy in knives, and at the beginning, small mistakes hurt less. If you start with $500 and buy five quality production knives at $100 each, you may enjoy them a long time. If you start with the same $500 and buy a custom at a show from an overhyped maker who quickly fades away, you may sour to collecting altogether. When you gamble more, the losses cost more.

The opposite is somewhat true as well, however. If you spend your $500 on 50 $10 gas station knives, you'll have a great big pile of crappy knives when you're done. The trick is finding a good balance between price and quality. Finding that balance takes time to learn.

As you learn more about the market segment you're interested in, don't be afraid to invest more as you grow. You may reach a point where you don't want the Chinese ones, but rather the American ones. Or maybe you don't want production, you want midtech. Or maybe you won't want the midtech one with the maker's name on it, you may want the custom one made by the maker himself.

Hopefully, your budget will grow to accommodate your growing expertise and preferences.

Lesson 3: It's Not Just The Knife You're Buying

When you invest in Amazon stock, you are making a rich man richer. You're buying a piece of paper or an electronic data point that says you "own" a tiny piece of the company, and you expect a mathematically increasing return for your investment.

When you buy a knife, odds are good your money won't go to that knifemaker's yacht payment or summer home fund. When you buy a knife from an individual knifemaker, you're more likely sending his kids to daycare or piano lessons, paying for his electricity and buying his wife new shoes. If you buy at a knife show, you probably bought the maker's dinner. When you invest in a knife, you support a specific person, not "the man behind the curtain."

Even if you find joy by investing in a person by buying their product, you still owe it to yourself to invest wisely. Of course, you should buy a knife you like, that you find useful or that may make you a decent return on your money. At the same time, you should be looking for

> While you may get a "great deal" from a pawn shop or somebody's cousin who is a knife collector, there is some measure of protection in buying from well-known retailers such as Blade HQ, AG Russell, Arizona Custom Knives and others.

people to help, individual makers whose lives you will improve by your relationship and the purchases you make over time. You may be making friends, not just money, which can add another degree of magnitude to your enjoyment of knife collecting.

Lesson 4:
Buy What You Know

The more you know, the fewer expensive mistakes you're likely to make and the more deals you're likely to find. The less you know, the more likely it is that you'll get a bad deal, purchase a knife you'll be dissatisfied with or a knife you later regret. The more you know, the better. This seems to be a universal principle of life and economics, and it applies to knives as well.

First off, buy knives from brands or people you know have a good market position. Many times, a well-known brand is successful for good reasons. A classic brand like Case or Spyderco may be a great place to start, or a well-known Knifemakers' Guild member or somebody from the "Slipjoint Cartel." When you have the chance to know the maker or seller personally, that knowledge makes your purchases more likely to bring you joy or a good return on your investment.

Second, buy knives from reputable dealers or purveyors. While you may get a "great deal" from a pawn shop or somebody's cousin who is a knife collector, there is some measure of protection in buying from well-known retailers such as Blade HQ, AG Russell, Arizona Custom Knives and others. Until you become familiar enough with the market to know exactly what you're looking at, it's wise to stick with the major dealers.

As another example, consider buying from the folks who advertise in the knife magazines, such as *BLADE*. If their business is legitimate enough to afford the expense of advertising in print, they're more likely to be honest and stick around.

Third, buy the knives you're familiar with. You may get joy out of buying a knife the first time you've ever seen or heard of it. On the other hand, you're even likelier to enjoy a knife that you know in your heart is a great one, because you've studied it, chased it, pursued it, and finally purchased after careful consideration. Sometimes the journey is as fun as the destination, and the pursuit of the grail is worth as much as the grail itself.

You may get in a rut and feel like you're buying the same knife over and over. That's no good either. Balance your knowledge with both width and depth. You may dive deep into one model, one maker or one brand, or you may spread your collection broadly by buying one knife from as many different people and places as possible. Either way, you'll get familiar with the knives that you like, and you'll end up going as deep or as broad in your collection as you like.

A Tale Of Two Knife Collectors

Let's wrap this up with two stories.

In one story, Bob buys a knife, then another, then another. He wanders aimlessly through the knife world throwing money everywhere. One day he wakes up and finds himself surrounded by knives that he doesn't like, knives of poor quality, knives he can't sell for a profit and knives that don't even cut. After his untimely death, his wife sells his whole collection for pennies on the dollar at a garage sale.

Was Bob a good knife collector? He may have found some joy in knives, and that's good. Other than that, he seems to have done poorly.

Larry, on the other hand, started as a hunter and purchased a custom knife to go with his hunting rifle. He then did some reading on custom knives and found a few makers whose styles he preferred. He bought knives for his sons and business partners, and then he started buying knives for his own collection.

Eventually, he found so much joy and knowledge in the knife world that he began to purchase knives that he knew were underpriced for their value. He kept good records of what he bought and from whom, and his spreadsheet included price paid and retail value. After his retirement, he gave the best of his collection to his boys and sold the rest at a handsome profit.

Was Larry a good knife collector? He seems to have been

knowledgeable and wise, and found both joy and profit in his collection. He died with zero knives to his name. He seems to have done very well.

When it comes to knife collecting, only you can decide what knives you like, what knives are "worth it" to pursue and purchase, and whether knife collecting adds to your overall joy in life. By carefully considering who and where you purchase from, by doing your own due diligence and by continual learning, you can have a wonderful knife collecting experience. ▲

CHAPTER 5

WHERE TO BUY COLLECTIBLE KNIVES IN PERSON

Let's first state the obvious: you can buy knives on the internet. However, I believe that "the internet" is too broad a description to be useful in this case. It's like asking your friend for where to by a nice, used Honda from an honest salesman, and your buddy says, "buy it at a car dealership."

"Buy knives on the internet" as advice is simultaneously true and nearly useless, so let's ignore it for now and talk about where one could buy a collectible knife in person.

Brick-And-Mortar Stores

The brick-and-mortar knife store market is awfully similar to the market for ribeye steaks. If you go to a "grocery" store, you can sometimes find ribeye steaks with mixed availability and mixed quality. Similarly, if you go to a big box retail or sporting goods store, you can sometimes find collectible knives with mixed availability and quality. You can at least find a usable knife at a big-box retailer, or maybe even a USA-made knife with quality materials.

If you have a taste for better

steaks, you may shop at a specialty grocery store with a meat market. In the knife world, this might be a gun store or high-end, brand name sporting goods store. You'll find fewer of the cheap junk knives, and the selection may push all the way up to midtechs or high-end production knives. If you want a dry-aged steak from a grass-fed Angus steer raised in Texas by a guy named Billy Bob and butchered on a Tuesday, you will end up at a specialty butcher shop. If you want similarly high-end knives, you'll find yourself shopping at a specialty knife store.

Let's dive in a bit more to the idea of specialty knife stores. On one side are high-end stores that carry a dedicated section of collectible knives. They may be gun stores, high-end clothing stores, fly fishing stores in tourist areas, among others.

I know of one local pharmacy that has a few showcases of customs, because the pharmacy owner's husband is a collector. I know of one in the basement of an antique store, which also carries $100,000 shotguns alongside high-end collectible custom knives. Another is an antique store that features antler chandeliers and other art, plus a half dozen cases of custom knives. Another is a specialty horsemanship store with ropes, tack, saddles and a very good gun and knife section. This type of store is not likely to have a website with much detail, but if you can find them, they are worth your time.

In the middle, I'd include stand alone and dedicated knife stores. These kinds of stores may just have the knives you won't be able to find anywhere else. Google "knife store" and the name of a city. You might also ask around.

There is some variety within this group, which includes low-end, "mall ninja"-type stores full of cheap imports, to generalist knife stores that might include factory, midtech and custom knives across several genres. Some of these stores may specialize in a certain genre, like tactical, culinary, hunting or collectible. They may be dedicated to one or two high end brands or may focus on regional customs from the makers nearby.

This category will have a website for sure, and perhaps an online catalog or online store. I'd consider House of Blades in Ft. Worth, Texas; Bear Claw Knife and Shear in Midland, Texas; and The Blade Bar in Grapevine, Texas, as excellent examples.

Finally, at the top of the knife brick-and-mortar retail world are the true specialty knife shops. They're few and far between, but there are some. This type of shop could be a destination in and of itself. They might host a knife show on the premises or specialize in nationally-known makers. They may have a solid online presence and offer high-end work on consignment.

One well known example was the recently closed Plaza Cutlery in California. The A.G. Russell store in Rogers, Arkansas, is anoth-

Plaza Cutlery is now closed, but check out the selection of knives in just this one photo. That is what a real-deal, specialty knife shop looks like.

er; as is Smoky Mountain Knife Works in Sevierville, Tennessee. Internationally, the famous Lorenzi store in Milan, Italy, is a great example.

Buy From The Guy!

One of the more reliable ways to get a collectible custom knife is to buy it direct from the knifemaker. This approach has several upsides, but a few challenges as well.

One of the best things about buying direct from makers is that you get to develop a relationship with them. You can talk to them face to face and get to know them on a personal level. As a maker, I love the opportunity to meet my customers face to face. I'm pretty likely to forget your name, lol, but I will for sure remember your face and the knife you bought for years to come.

Another benefit to buying direct from the maker is the potential for truly custom work. If you buy from the store, you may not get the handle color you want or the exact blade shape. If you buy from the maker and can explain in person the exact knife you want, you can get just that. You want a bowie, you can ask for one. You want blue mammoth ivory, you can get it.

Many successful makers sell their work directly at prices well below the secondary market. If you have a dealer as a middleman, they deserve a commission or a return on their investment, and they include that in their price. Very few makers reach for the secondary market pricing on individual sales.

Buying direct is not all rainbows and butterflies. One major downside is availability. If you buy a knife at a store or off a website, you get it quickly, if not immediately. If you buy from a maker, you're limited to the knives they have on hand. If you order a knife from a maker, you may end up waiting a long time until your knife is ready. The waitlist for a reputable maker may be not months, but *years*.

Another challenge to buying direct is makers with poor business practices. If they take money in advance and don't deliver on time, that's a problem. If they won't communicate, that's a problem. An individual knifemaker may not have as many checks and balances as a larger business or established dealer.

Knife Show And Tell

Some people in the knife world argue that knife shows are past their prime. Even if we acknowledge that a knife show today is different than the major Guild shows of the 1980s and 1990s, for example, that certainly doesn't mean that knife shows are no good anymore.

Let's do a little history lesson for the newcomers. Once up on a time, there were no knife shows. In the early 1970s, some makers worked together to host groups of tables at gun shows. Eventually, one such group of makers coalesced into the Knifemakers' Guild. By the 1980s, the Guild hosted a major show every year.

Through the '80s and '90s, the Guild show was *the* top-end knife show in the world. If you wanted a knife from Buster Warenski, Gil Hibben, Bob Loveless, Steve Johnson, D'Alton Holder, Ron Lake or many of the other greats, the Guild show was the best place to get one. I've heard stories of makers selling $50-$75,000 worth of knives in a weekend and making their whole year's income at a single show, but I am not the one to tell those stories. Find the oldest knifemaker you know and ask them how shows used to be.

In the 1990s, there was a major technological shift that changed the knife world: a little invention known as "the internet." Knives became available in new ways,

Another benefit to buying direct from the maker is the potential for truly custom work. If you buy from the store, you may not get the handle color you want or the exact blade shape. If you buy from the maker and can explain in person the exact knife you want, you can get just that.

> One advantage of the local gun show approach to knife buying is that you never know when you'll find a great deal.

___

including direct email lists, consignment and dealer websites, and makers' personal websites.

Now, the internet is everywhere, and we all carry in our pockets the knowledge of humanity on our smartphones. We'll come back to the internet later, though, as this section is about knife shows. It's impossible to deny the impact the internet has on the evolution of the knife show industry.

Knife shows come in several varieties. Kind of like the proverbial box of chocolates, you never know what you're gonna get when you go.

At one end of the spectrum are the local "gun and knife" shows. They're in towns large and small, and may have 50 or 100 tables. They may be in a VFW hall, a community center or a civic center auditorium. In a show like this, you may just find a "real live" knifemaker.

Many successful makers sell knives at the local shows near where they live. American Bladesmith Society (ABS) master smith Harvey Dean tells a story

The Knifemakers' Guild was key in bringing knife shows to the world. Here's a look at Mel Pardue (right) and Bob Sims (left) from a Guild show in the 1980s. (Image courtesy of the Knifemakers' Guild.)

The **BLADE** Show takes place every year in Atlanta. You'll never meet as many knife enthusiasts under one roof anywhere else in the world.

about going to a ho-hum, regular old knife show in Waco, Texas, in the 1990s. He sold a couple of knives--nothing spectacular—but at that show he met a customer who later bought over $25,000 worth of Harvey's knives over the next 20 years. Knifemakers and

In the United States, the biggest and best knife show is BLADE Show. BLADE Show is your one-stop shop for almost everything the knife world has to offer.

customers are where you find them!

One advantage of the local gun show approach to knife buying is that you never know when you'll find a great deal. You may find a custom or collectible knife on almost any table, scattered among the AR-15 parts, antique and modern guns, and various ammunition.

Another variety of show is the regional show. There are dedicated "knife shows" scattered throughout the country. I've been to a 15-maker knife show in a barbecue restaurant, and a 150-maker show in the corner of a 1,000-table gun show. There are quality regional knife shows in all parts of the country. These shows will often feature makers who are well known on the national and even international level, who attend the regional show nearest where they live. These shows may also have a dealer or knife manufacturing company presence, and are often a good place for knifemakers to buy supplies.

Beyond the regional shows, there are just a few shows that truly reach the national level. The original Guild show partnered with the American Bladesmith Society to put on the International Custom Cutlery Expo (ICCE), which after a six-year independent run is now a regional affiliate of the BLADE show. The Art Knife Invitational is a true, high-end, national knife show. The Usual Suspects Network Gathering is a national-level show that highlights the best that the modern folding and tactical genre has to offer.

In the United States, the biggest and best knife show is BLADE Show. BLADE Show is your one-stop shop for almost everything the knife world has to offer. There are hundreds of tables of every kind of custom knife you can imagine, including the best national and international knifemakers. There are booths by all of the major vendors of equipment and supplies, as well as dealers of production knives, and various dealers and purveyors.

BLADE Show has been around since 1982, first taking place in Ft. Mitchell, Kentucky. In 1992, the show moved to Atlanta, Georgia, and has been there ever since. By 1997, the show was big enough to move to the Cobb Galleria.

As of this writing, BLADE Show has more than 900 different knife-specific exhibits. Attendance is regularly well above 10,000.

BLADE expanded with a reboot of the BLADE Show West show in 2018 and BLADE Show Texas (the former ICCE show) beginning in 2021. These shows bring the same level of excellence from both the maker and show production side to smaller regional venues. These shows are relatively smaller but still feature 200 to 300 exhibitors of the highest quality.

A final thing to consider about knife shows is the whole experience. While knife shows are clearly places you can get a knife, a knife show offers more than just a purchasing opportunity. Where else can you visit with multiple knifemakers face to face? Where else can you comparison shop? Where else can you hang out after the sale and socialize? Where else can you see such variety of product, from $50 production up through $50,000 customs?

If you're new to BLADE Show, you may not know about "The Pit,"

the after-hours social time with adult beverages and knife shenanigans that occurs in the show hotel. Even if the social scene isn't your thing, the networking opportunities alone are worth the experience.

If you think of a knife show as simply a place to buy a knife, you're missing some of the unique goodness that a show has to offer. ▲

CHAPTER 6

BUYING KNIVES ON THE INTERNET

In the previous chapter, I poked a little fun at the simplicity of the idea that you can buy collectible knives on the internet. This is deceivingly simple, so let's break it down a bit.

Hit The Websites

Let's start with the most obvious: go to your preferred search engine, type in the name of the knife or knifemaker you're looking for and go to their personal or business website.

As a one-off knifemaker, I have a website that serves as a catalog of my work, a point of contact for potential customers, sales of my books and a sign-up portal for my mailing list. Some makers go so far as to directly sell their knives from their personal website, although this is not very common. It is almost cliché that custom knifemakers have mediocre websites.

Would you expect the IT guy at your job to be an excellent knifemaker? Probably not, even if he's an excellent IT guy. In the same way, you may not be surprised to find that many competent and even excellent knifemakers are not all that good at web development. Many individual knifemakers' websites are outdated, poorly designed or just all-around crappy. In the same way you wouldn't judge your IT guy by his knifemaking, don't fall to the temptation to judge a knifemakers' work by his website alone.

> Many individual knifemakers' websites are outdated, poorly designed or just all-around crappy. In the same way you wouldn't judge your IT guy by his knifemaking, don't fall to the temptation to judge a knifemakers' work by his website alone.

A quality website for an individual knifemaker should have a brief bio, pictures of recent work and up to date contact information. It's just as likely that the bio will be several years old or that the contact information will be missing or out of date. Most knifemakers' websites are simply an initial point of contact, an internet billboard that points you toward an in-person or email conversation.

For many knifemakers, when they have time to work on knife stuff, they want to be in the shop building knives. Is it great business to let your website languish? Of course not, but as a maker I certainly understand why it happens. As a knife buyer, I hope you'll understand, and that you won't judge the quality of a maker's work by their website alone.

You should expect a knife manufacturing company to have a website. Many of the major knife manufacturers distribute exclusively through dealer websites. Unlike the one-off and hobby knifemakers, these companies have the resources to hire a competent professional to do their web development. Those makers, manufacturers and dealers who take making money seriously will have quality websites almost every time.

The Deal With Dealers

When you buy a knife from Blade HQ, direct from Case or another quality dealer, you get the familiar internet purchasing experience. You see what's in stock, typically in a series of stock photos, add it to your "cart" and pay online.

These types of dealers are reliable and predictable, in that they have good financial security, good inventory management, and a well-established shipping procedure. If you're afraid of internet scams or hackers, start your internet knife experience at a quality dealer. Buy a knife to carry, just to

A. G. Russell's List of Knives for Immediate Delivery

June, 1985

1705 Hiway 71 North • Springdale, Arkansas 72764
Telephone 501-751-7341

All the knives in this list are in unused condition unless we say they have been used. All straight knives have sheaths unless we say not.

GUARANTEE

ANY KNIFE YOU ORDER FROM THE LIST MAY BE RETURNED WITHIN 14 DAYS FOR FULL REFUND OR CREDIT.

The best way to order is by phone, we can charge your selection to your Master Charge or Visa card, or will hold it until your check arrives. Next best is send your order by mail with a second choice in case the first is already gone.

These lists are a marketing service for knife collectors. We take these knives on consignment from collectors. Our selling commission is 25%.

These lists are mailed 1st class to subscribers who have paid $5.00 for one year, $9.50 for two years, or $13.00 for three years. They are mailed 3rd class to all members of The Knife Collectors Club who have paid for a membership or knife in the past year. OVERSEAS SUBSCRIBERS MUST ADD $5.00 A YEAR FOR AIR MAIL POSTAGE - OVERSEAS BUYERS MUST ALSO PAY EXTRA FOR AIR SHIPMENTS.

U.S.: Add $3.00 per knife for shipping and handling.
CANADA & MEXICO: Add $6.75 per knife for shipping and handling for registered air mail.
OTHER COUNTRIES: Add $10.00 per knife for AIR MAIL.

We have collectors who have been buying from and selling through these lists since 1970, we have collectors in almost every country outside the Soviet Block. If you are not already using these lists to build your collection you should be. Our prices are fair and our guarantee is solid.

TELEPHONE 501-751-7341   8:00 a.m. - 5:00 p.m. CST

2615. PUMA Ltd Edition only 1769 for entire world here are four low serial numbers at rock bottom prices all with presentation boxes	
#13	$345.00
#122	$295.00
#139.00	$285.00
#262	$255.00
2617. KRESSLER Damascus blade cocobolo handle brass hilt & butt very fine, very low price	$595.00
2618. KRESSLER Damascus folder #104 one of only 5 made low price	$295.00
2619. KRESSLER Damascus hunter rose damascus African Blackwood handle n/s hilt and butt very low price	$695.00
2620. AG RUSSELL HEN & ROOSTER Bicentennial Set of less than 20 these very fine embossed pocket knives are priced at about half of market price	$995.00
2622. GERBER Presentation FS II engraved by Geo Sherwood etched blade in walnut box very low price	$85.00
2627. McCARTY 7" Bowie with black micarta scales and brass hilt	$110.00
2636. FUNDERBURG 4" push dagger ivory micarta	$155.00
2645. RUFFIN JOHNSON 11½" kukri #13 with brass hilt butt spacer and inlay no sheath very low price	$295.00
2651. HEN & ROOSTER CM-5 Whittler 3½" closed ebony handle serial No. 50 Only 1200 total made. The rarest of all Cm knives. The excelsior grade engraved and gold etched blade, Bargain at	$195.00
2653. HEN & ROOSTER CM-5 serial No. 619. 3½" closed. Whittler with ebony handle. Mint	$125.00
2660. GODDARD No. 0-1 steel with burgandy micarta handle. Belt Pouch	$195.00
2663. BONE 3" model V No. 220, 7½" overal bird & trout wit exotic hardwood & brass. Used	$70.00

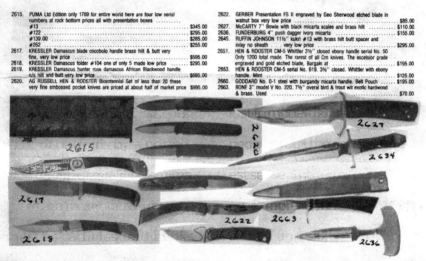

Arkansas businessman A.G. Russell essentially created the custom knife secondary market. Beginning in 1968, he sent out *AG Russell's List of Knives for Immediate Delivery*, which has evolved into today's *Cutting Edge Catalog*. (Images courtesy of A.G. Russell Knives.)

The Cutting Edge®

KLSP91135
Walker

KLSP91112
Lucie

KLSP91179
Moran

KLSP91117
Pease

KLSP91148
Collins

Pre-Owned and Handmade Knives
for Immediate Delivery
January 2022

break the ice. You'll have a good experience.

Other knife dealers specialize in consignment. In this scenario, a maker or collector pays a percentage to the company, and the company does all the work of marketing and selling. The major consignment houses like A.G. Russell, Arizona Custom Knives or Knife Legends are among the most reliable ways to get a custom knife from a long-time or deceased maker.

Arkansas businessman A.G. Russell essentially created the custom knife secondary market. Beginning in 1968, he sent out *AG Russell's List of Knives for Immediate Delivery*, which has evolved into today's *Cutting Edge Catalog*.

On the upside, this is a good business model where the risk to the buyer is low, and these types tend to specialize in hard-to-find customs. On the downside, you'll pay a little more. The middleman is entitled to his percentage of the deal. Typically, the initial seller bears part of the percentage by discounting the price, but the buyer pays a premium as well.

Individual Sellers

For the true adventurer, there are some other options. Much like the Wild West or the current crypto-currency market, dealing with individual sellers can be great or can be a minefield. It depends primarily on the character of the individuals involved.

Since it's the internet and by

nature a bit anonymous, the potential for "bad guys" is much greater. However, the potential for a great deal or a "grail" knife is also much greater.

If you're ready, here are some of the usual places to find individual sellers.

Ebay

Occasionally, a knife you want will pop up on eBay. Rather than compulsively checking every day to see if anything new is listed, you can search for your favorite terms and then add the term to your "saved searches." To save a search term, click the heart icon that says, "save this search." From that point forward, when any new listings are posted that match your search criteria, you will get an email notification. This system works well for knives you don't see often online.

For example, my saved search for "Jason Fry knife" has yet to yield one of my knives for sale on eBay in several years, but the first time there's one up, I'll see it. On the other hand, this would not be a good system to use to search for a Chris Reeve knife or Case knife or some other knife that's readily available elsewhere.

Bladeforums Classifieds

Another good option is the classified forums on some of the major knife websites. While Usual Suspects Network and others are good examples, I'll talk you through Blade Forums as the exemplar.

Bladeforums.com is the largest and one of the oldest knife forums on the web. Among its features is a robust classified section. In one area called the Knife Exchange, you can find dozens of brand-specific classifieds, knives for sale by dealers, and knives for sale by individual collectors. The classifieds are broken down by type: folder, fixed blade, etc.

A nice associated feature of this classified system is a forum called, "Feedback: The Good, The Bad, The Ugly," which contains stories of both good and bad deals between individuals. If you're concerned about the individual you're considering purchasing from, check them out in the feedback section.

Another good sub-group of the Knife Exchange is the Knifemakers'

Market. Within this section you can find knives for sale directly from the knifemakers. To sell on Bladeforums, a maker must register as a Knifemaker Member and pay a yearly fee. This tends to weed out the riffraff.

One of the primary tools on the Bladeforums classified system is the search feature. This feature lets you hunt for a specific model or maker to view not only currently available knives, but also threads about knives that have already been sold. Browsing the "sold" threads is a good way to learn about pricing and the amount of volume in the market you're looking at.

One challenge to Bladeforums is the sheer volume of knives available. There are quite a few subsections, and certain sections move very quickly, with dozens of posts per day. In a quick-moving forum, you can certainly miss opportunities. At the same time, opportunities come fast, and the market is unregulated, so you just might find a knife that's priced below market value.

Good deals are available for those who search diligently, and bad deals are avoidable for those who learn their market niche.

... the major social media platforms of Facebook and Instagram actively try to keep knives from being sold on their platforms. If you search "knives for sale," you won't find anything.

Social Media

Social media changes quickly. I almost hesitate to write about it, because things might be different by the time this goes to print. With that caveat, dive in.

First things first: the major social media platforms of Facebook and Instagram actively try to keep knives from being sold on their platforms. If you search "knives for sale," you won't find anything. If you post a knife in a formal marketplace, it'll get taken down every time. If you use #knifesale on

> I've sold two or three knives on social media in the last year, but at least 30 to my email list. My email list gets advance notice of availability, special deals and hears about upcoming shows and events.

Instagram, don't expect it to do anything for you. Knife dealing on these platforms is more of an under-the-table enterprise.

The thing about selling on Instagram and Facebook is choosing your words carefully so that you can avoid their filters. Simple things like "for sale" or "available" will get flagged, and so what you'll often see is some version of "message for details." I'd go so far to say that "message for details" is straight up internet code for "this item is for sale." Using the direct messenger feature, you contact the seller, and the deal is finalized.

Another trick that works on Facebook (as of this writing) is to post a picture and details, and then add the price and sale details in the comments. It seems as if the algorithm searches the main posts but doesn't screen the comments as heavily.

Many makers and knife companies have dedicated Facebook

user groups or Instagram profiles. This is a good way to keep track of what is going on in terms of new products, upcoming product drops, etc. You simply follow the companies or makers you're interested in, and their content shows up in your feed. Those who are less serious may only have a personal profile, not a second profile just for the business.

There are also private buy/sell/trade or auction groups dedicated to some knife companies. Some specific genres (like cowboy knives, everyday carry knives, art knives, etc.) have their own groups as well. In these groups, items are routinely bought and sold, and for some reason the algorithm is less strict in a private group than on a user feed.

Neither Facebook nor Instagram are particularly kind to links, so you won't often find a link to a makers' website or to a knife for sale. Google owns YouTube and is a direct competitor of Facebook and Instagram, and so video links are routinely de-emphasized. Instagram doesn't allow links at all, even in the comments.

Email: Not As Cool, But Still Effective

I remember back in 1996 when I first went to college and got email. Web browsers were new at the time also, and you had to go to a MS DOS page to login to the email system.

Fast forward 25 years, and we have email and the internet on the phones in our pockets. My wife's

93-year-old grandmother now has email. Many knifemakers and quality businesses will have an email list. You simply sign up via their website, and when something worth knowing comes along, they'll send it to your inbox. Because of the anti-spam laws, these subscriptions come with an easy "unsubscribe" button, so you can literally quit at any time.

Speaking only from my personal experience, I've sold two or three knives on social media in the last year, but at least 30 to my email list. My email list gets advance notice of availability, special deals and hears about upcoming shows and events.

Just like at a knife show, buying direct from the maker when they have knives available allows you to pay a fair price, to get to know the maker a little bit and to directly reward the craftsman (or woman) responsible for the creation you're purchasing. ▲

SO, YOU WANT TO BUY A CUSTOM KNIFE?

T he world of custom knives can be confusing and difficult to understand. In this section, we show you some examples of creations that you'll find from custom makers, with features that'll make your heart palpitate.

Photo by SharpByCoop

Moran - When Bill Moran re-introduced damascus steel to the modern world of custom knives, it was absolutely revolutionary. Since then, the art of pattern welding has progressed far beyond what Moran could have imagined.

Photo by SharpByCoop

Laurent - When most people think of a knife, they think of the ones in their kitchen, their pocket or their hunting pack. Belgian master smith Veronique Laurent pushes the limits of knife design with this folding dagger, "Little Adrienne." When you think about buying a "knife," the possibilities are endless.

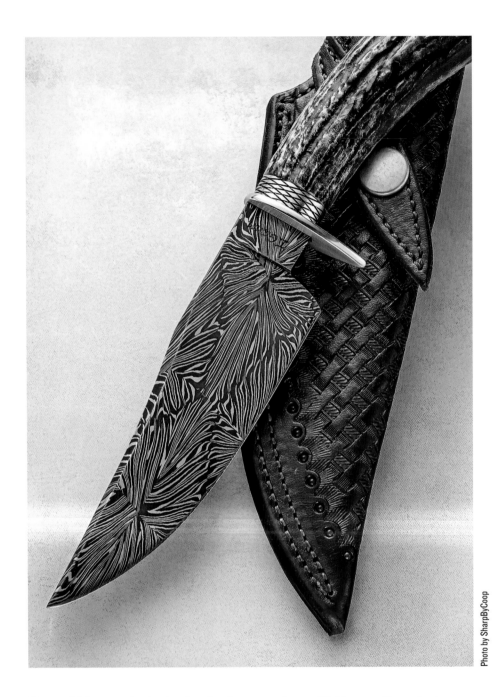

Photo by SharpByCoop

Gann - This award-winning hunter from master smith Tommy Gann features a mosaic damascus pattern similar to the one sketched in Chapter 9.

Rexford - At first glance, this Todd Rexford folder has a standard drop-point blade with a flat grind and an eye-catching flowing profile. Look closer and you'll notice the complexity of the handle design, made of multi-piece titanium and stainless steel. It's no wonder his knives are in high demand.

Photo by SharpByCoop

Terzuola - Check out the variety in this group of knives by the legendary Bob Terzuola. If you're fluent in materials identification, you'll see musk ox, mokume, Timascus, carbon fiber, zirconium, vintage micarta and some kind of African horn. Note also the variety of blade materials: multiple patterns of damascus including damascus clad over a monosteel core, and a monosteel blade with selective coatings. There is great variety in blade shapes and grinds as well.

Photo by SharpByCoop

Stubblefield - Don't overlook kitchen knives as a high-end collectible category. This fine piece from Brent Stubblefield at Join or Die Knives has a multi-bar mosaic damascus blade, integral bolster, mammoth tooth spacer and koa handle. Features include a handle shape modeled after the Sabatier knives, and an "S-grind," where the middle of the blade is hollow ground while the edge is flat ground. There were nine separate forge welds required for this knife.

Shirogorov - This high-end folding knife by the Shirogorov brothers features a compound grind. Look closely at the plunge area. Notice how the knife has both a full flat grind and a Scandi or saber grind at the same time.

Kolenko - We've become a bit familiar with the TV standard of "it will cut" and "it will keel." Pennsylvania knifemaker Vladimir Kolenko pushed the standard far beyond simple performance with this exceptional art dagger, 21 inches long with a sail-shaped guard.

Osborne - If you take a knife that's already worth thousands, and then add thousands more in engraving and gold work, you end up with a top-shelf knife like this exceptional art piece from Warren Osborne engraved by Simone Fezzardi.

Photo by SharpByCoop

Loerchner - Wolfgang Loerchner is a long-time art knife maker with unmistakable style. He is a good example of a maker whose knives may be available on consignment or through dealers on the secondary market. This trio was sold through Knife Legends.

Photo by SharpByCoop

Appleton - When it comes to top-of-the-line fit and finish, it doesn't get much better than Ron Appleton. Even with all the complexity of the swirling pivot and the fluted grinds, the symmetry and finish of this piece is flawless.

Image Edit by Jocelyn Frasier

Lin Rhea - Master smith Lin Rhea combines old-school blacksmithing skills with innovative design techniques. Each of the fittings on this knife are forged precisely to shape. It's hard to believe Lin can do all that with a hammer!

Zieba - Notice the different grinds on this fine pair of flippers from Michael Zieba. While both are his "MS4" model, the one on the left features a dagger grind and a fuller, while the one on the right has a full flat grind.

Begg - This folding knife, called the "Bodega," from Todd Begg features anodized titanium and a compound hollow grind. A semi-custom from his shop in California prior to his move to Texas, this one was undoubtedly somebody's "grail." Todd says it's named after Bodega Bay near his old shop, not a New York corner store.

Regel - The bowie knife is an American icon, but makers the world over have put their spin on it. This award-winning bowie from French master smith Jean-Louis Regel fits squarely in the genre, and features world-class mosaic damascus and a forged D-guard.

CHAPTER 7

WHAT KNIFE COLLECTOR PERSONALITY ARE YOU?

Have you ever taken one of those personality tests online or at work, like a Myers-Briggs, StrengthsFinder or Enneagram? You end up with a description of your personality tendencies, and invariably some of them are exactly how you see yourself.

While I have the nerd skills to put together a knife collector personality test like that, I don't think it would be that useful. Instead, I'll skip straight to the results and describe a few varieties of the "knife collector personality." Maybe something in one of these descriptions will resonate with you.

The Accidental Collector

Collectors in this category are buying and accumulating knives because those knives do certain tasks well. They're not afraid to buy a knife for one specific purpose and may find themselves in possession of more knives than they realized they had.

I got my first knife at around age 7; a small Case folder. This knife, like many others I've owned, was used and then lost. Fast forward

34 years, and I still use a knife. I started making knives because I didn't have enough sharp knives to accommodate the tasks I was engaged in at the time. I hunt and use a knife to process my deer and other game animals. I use knives in the kitchen. I skin fish, slice vegetables and open packages. I carry a small Swiss army knife with me on my keychain. Am I a knife collector?

Am I a knife collector? In my mind I am not a "knife collector," but I figure I might be after all. You might be an Accidental Collector, too, and not even know it.

Just for kicks while pondering this question, I took a quick inventory. I have three custom and two quality production knives in my kitchen. I have five customs in my hunting pack, not counting the ones my sons have. I've got three or four spare keychain knives. I started a minor collection on purpose once and acquired 10 or 12 trapper pattern slipjoints and a few vintage folding knives in other patterns before I decided I wasn't a collector, but I still have the knives.

In addition, I've got various junk knives stashed around in cars, trucks, shops and drawers, including the usual assortment of junk kitchen knives from big box marts, plus all the decent ones that I forgot where I put them. By quick count, I've got about a dozen customs and another 75 production knives.

Am I a knife collector? In my mind I am not a "knife collector," but I figure I might be after all. You might be an Accidental Collector, too, and not even know it.

The Investor

Collectors of this type always have an eye on the bottom line. They're familiar with the primary and secondary markets, and can instantly spot a good deal. They are always looking for the "next big thing," the knife that is not hot yet but will be soon. They know the value of "buy low, sell high," but they also watch which makers and knives appreciate over time.

Some folks invest in stocks or real estate, while others apply their knife knowledge as part of an investment strategy.

I think of my friend Jimmy McMahon as an example of this category. I remember back in 2010 when he invited me to my very first knife show. At the time, he was proud of a knife he had just purchased from Kyle Royer, then a 19-year-old journeyman smith. Given Kyle's continued improvement and his current status in the industry, I'd say Jimmy made a good investment. If Jimmy were to sell that knife today, he'd make a handsome profit.

The Philanthropist/ Helper

Have you ever met a person who was a real people-person and just

Some folks invest in stocks or real estate, while others apply their knife knowledge as part of an investment strategy.

---

wanted to help everyone? When a person like this collects knives, they continue with that approach.

Some collectors buy from makers they know and have a relationship with. Some buy from makers whose story they know, makers for whom the buyer knows that every single sale makes a difference. These collectors may be biased toward purchasing from makers who are newer, younger or less well established.

One fairly well-known example is knifemaker Lloyd Hale. Lloyd disappeared from the knifemaking scene in the early 1980s, only to re-appear 20 years later. Lloyd tucked away for all that time in his shop working for his patron, Owsley Brown Frazier. Lloyd created over 300 knives, daggers and swords for Owsley, who just happened to be one of the country's premier gun and arms collectors. Many of these knives along with a great number of historical pieces are on display in the Frazier Museum in Louisville, Kentucky.

Another good example is my friend, David Smith. He loves to talk, to share what he has and a good knife. Over the years as

I developed in the craft, he has purchased 6 or 8 pieces from me. He's given some as gifts, but all have been put to use.

One story stands out as a great illustration of David's character and the Philanthropist/Helper.

One of my first forged knives was made from the tooth of a drag harrow that came from my grandfather's farm. I'd held onto the tooth for many years until my forging skills were up to the task. The knife also included wrought iron and some figured red oak milled in 1955 that was recovered during a remodel from the floor of my house at the time.

Even though this knife was tied to me in many ways, with two small kids at home I found myself in an economic pinch, so I had to put the knife out for sale. I priced it at what was for me a high price at the time, and David snatched it right up. He also promised to give me the knife back when he passed away.

About four years later, I was able to travel across country and again visit David at his hunting camp where we used to hang out 15 years prior. True to his word, David gave me back the knife, saying that he didn't want his wife to have to figure out where to send all the stuff he'd promised folks after he died. He's almost died four or five times in the last 20 years, but as of this writing is still alive and well. I've since adopted that knife as one of my primary using knives, and it's a treasure I'll never part with.

The Art Appreciator

These people love art for art's sake, who take the time to stop and admire the roses, who simply enjoy having beautiful things around them. That there would be people like this who gravitate toward knives-as-art is no real surprise. Just like those who collect paintings, sculptures or any other kind of art, these people buy knives simply to appreciate their beauty and the skillful craftsmanship that went into their creation.

I never met David Darom, but with some familiarity with his books, I assume he was an Art Appreciator. His books feature the best knives in the world from a variety of genres, from top makers both stateside and international. If you're not familiar with his work, The Great Collections is a good place to start.

I remember as an incoming probationary member at the Guild Show in 2013 hearing a buzz in the room when a $30,000 knife was sold by Warren Osborne. As a young guy in the back row, I had no idea what kind of knife would bring that kind of price, nor what kind of customer would buy one. I later saw the knife, with gold and fine engraving on a damascus interframe folder. My guess is that it was purchased by an Art Appreciator.

There are a few fine examples of this kind of knife in the center photo section.

The "Squirrel!" Collector

Some readers will recognize

the "Squirrel!" reference from the Disney movie Up. It's a great illustration of the ADHD/impulsivity that goes along with some personality types, mine included. This type of collector simply buys knives that they like at the moment. Rather than a systematic approach, it's more like "here a knife, there a knife, everywhere a knife knife!"

While some might argue that this isn't a "real" collecting strategy, I believe that if it's enjoyable to the collector, then it's a legitimate pursuit. Even so, these stories don't always turn out well.

My fishing buddy, Cliff, is a good example. He asked me once to sharpen his knives prior to an elk hunting trip. What he brought me was an imported Buck folder, a decent Benchmade fixed blade and two no-name folding knives from Bass Pro. Each one sharpened differently, and each was designed for a different purpose. None of them were well suited to skinning an elk. Cliff was happy to share them with me and glad for me to sharpen them, but no elk were harmed on his hunting adventure.

The Historical/ Sentimental Collector

Some collectors specialize in history of one kind or another. Maybe they collect only Case "tested" knives like their grandpa or father carried. Maybe they have a collection of knives directly from their ancestors, or connected to a specific historical event (e.g.

Civil War), a specific era (e.g. the American West) or an international genre that connects with their heritage. For these collectors, part of the value of the knife is the connection that it makes with something both personal and historical.

Some collectors specialize in history of one kind or another. Maybe they collect only Case "tested" knives like their grandpa or father carried. Maybe they have a collection of knives directly from their ancestors, or connected to a specific historical event ...

Master smith Jerry Fisk targets this kind of collector with his high-end bowies that include historical materials. He's made knives from World Trade Center steel. He's used wood from trees planted by George Washington. He's made damascus with one layer for every person in the United States.Elements from Thomas Jefferson, Dr. Mudd, the Liberty Bell, the Alamo and Pearl Harbor have been worked into Fisk knives over the years. When a collector buys these knives, they're buying a connection to a story, not just a knife.

My friend, David Patterson, of League City, Texas, fits this category. He's been collecting knives for many years and has a great collection of the work of knifemakers from the 60s and 70s like Merle Seguine, Clyde Fischer, Gordon and Ruffin Johnson, Randall and Moreseth. He also has a long-standing collection of a knife from every single master smith in Arkansas.

The Grail Seeker

There's a personality type that loves the thrill of the hunt, for whom the journey is as important as the destination. These folks love to get the hottest new thing, or pursue the rarest or most sought-after knives. If you follow the trends and buy at the peak, you may be this kind of collector.

The market depends somewhat on people willing to play this role. The thrill of the acquisition can be as important as the knife itself. These folks developed the term "grail" knife, that knife for which you'd forsake all others, the knife at the top of the pinnacle.

It's All About The Knives

Whatever your personal reasons for collecting, and whatever personality traits encourage you down the path you've chosen, we all share one thing in common: the love of the knife. ▲

CHAPTER 8

A COLLECTOR'S GUIDE TO KNIFE STEEL

Saying that a knife is made of "steel" is like going into Starbucks and asking for a cup of coffee. It's true, but there are so many varieties. In fact, collectors new and seasoned can get confused. Don't worry if you're one of them. This chapter will help you understand what types of steel should be used for what purposes, and hopefully that will help you make a more educated decision on which steel to choose.

Making Steel Is Like Baking A Cake

A cake takes flour, sugar and eggs. What goes into steel? At the simplest level, steel is a combination of iron and carbon. Over time, metallurgists discovered that adding different elements to this basic steel recipe can adjust the toughness, hardness, wear resistance and corrosion resistance of the final product. The combinations of these added elements account for most of the difference between types of steel in blades.

There are advantages and disadvantages to each added element. For example, a certain alloy might make a blade harder. The harder the steel, the longer it will hold its edge. However, a

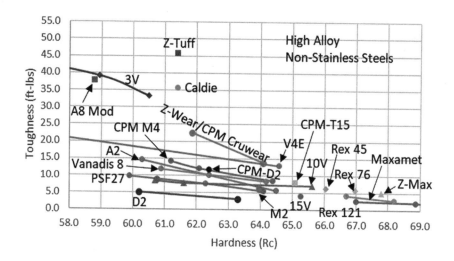

A look at the properties of different stainless alloys. (Image courtesy of Larrin Thomas/Knifesteelnerds.com)

blade with higher hardness is less tough, which means the blade is less resistant to shock and impact. Unfortunately, a blade cannot be simultaneously harder *and* tougher. As you add toughness, you make the blade less hard and vice versa.

What's a metallurgist to do? They tweak the recipe for varying characteristics. Each proportion and each alloying element change some property in the balance, improving one and decreasing another.

A Quick Guide to Alloy Elements

Let's take a look at some of the basic alloy elements and their functions.

Carbon - This ingredient makes the difference between iron and steel: all steel will have some amount of carbon. It is the most important hardening element, but it makes hardness by combining with other elements. As a simple generalization, the amount of carbon in the steel tells you a lot about the quality of the steel. Low carbon steel has 0.3% carbon or less, medium has between 0.4-0.7% and high-carbon steel is 0.8% and above, maxing out at around 1.2% carbon for knife

---

The harder the steel, the longer it will hold its edge. However, a blade with higher hardness is less tough, which means the blade is less resistant to shock and impact.

steels. Up to a point, the higher the carbon content within the range, the harder the steel will get.

Chromium – Chromium combines with carbon to make chromium carbides, which are resistant to corrosion. Stainless steel knives will have chromium as a major ingredient, typically at a minimum of 12-13%. Chromium also increases the strength of a knife to a degree, but adding chromium in large amounts decreases toughness.

Cobalt – In small amounts, cobalt increases toughness.

Manganese – This changes the rate of hardening. Manganese in carbon steels yields "deeper" hardening, which requires a slower speed quench and gives a wider range of acceptable heat prior to quench. If added in high quantities, it can increase brittleness. Manganese makes steel etch dark in damascus.

Molybdenum – Adding this maintains the steel's strength at high temperatures.

Nickel – Nickel adds toughness to steel. It also makes steel etch bright in damascus.

Nitrogen - This element is sometimes used as a substitute for carbon in steel.

Silicon – Silicon increases strength and removes oxygen from the metal while it is being formed. It's typically present in small quantity in most steels.

Sulfur – This increases machinability but decreases toughness.

Tungsten – Adding this increases wear resistance and forms tungsten carbides that are very hard.

Vanadium – Vanadium leads to smaller grains within the steel. Vanadium carbides are very small and hard, which increases wear resistance and edge retention.

Types Of Steel

There are literally thousands of types of steel. Among them, the most common categories used in knives are carbon steels, alloy steels, tool steels and stainless steels.

Each of these types of steel has a designation system that gives them a specific number, but these designations vary somewhat by system.

As an example, in the SAE (Society of Automotive Engineers) designation system, carbon steel and alloy steel are designated by a four-digit number, where the first digit indicates the main element, the second digit indicates the secondary element and the last two digits indicate the amount of carbon, in hundredths of a percent by weight. This means that 1095 steel would be .95% carbon.

In addition, in the SAE system any steel starting with a letter is classified as tool steel.

Carbon Steels

Plain carbon steels are steels that contain iron, carbon and a small amount of manganese. In contrast, alloy steels have a specified composition and contain certain percentages of vanadium or molybdenum, and they also typically have a larger amount of manganese.

The 10xx (1045-1095) Steels - 1095 and 1084 are the most common 10XX steel (or "high carbon" steel) used for knife blades. Steel in the range 1060-1095 are used for knife blades, although 1050 is more commonly seen in swords. In general, within this category, the higher the carbon content (the last two numbers represented by the XX in the designation), the higher the final hardness and wear resistance. The major drawback to this type of steel is that it rusts easily. Because of this issue, you will often see production 1095 blades, such as on an ESSE knife, come with some type of coating to combat rust. If you buy a knife with a 10-series blade, be sure to maintain it well and you should have no problem.

Also, occasionally, carbon, alloy and tool steels will be designated "carbon steel" because these steels will rust, whereas stainless steels are much more corrosion resistant.

Alloy Steels

5160 Steel - This is plain carbon steel (1060) that has been mixed with a little bit of chromium. There is not enough chromium to make it a stainless steel, but the chromium has been added to strengthen the material. This type of steel is known for its outstanding toughness. This type of steel typically has .56-.64% carbon. 5160 is a good forging steel and has a fairly simple heat treat procedure. It will rust if neglected.

Many other steels in this catego-ry are not suitable for knifemaking, but you will occasionally see 8670 mentioned as a knife steel. 4140 is a popular steel for hammers and impact tools.

Tool Steels

Tool steel contains tungsten, molybdenum and other alloying elements.

52100 Steel - This is high-carbon tool steel. It typically has .98-1.10% carbon. This steel can be hardened to a higher hardness than many others, and conse-quently it holds an edge well. This is one of the best carbon steels to use if you are worried about holding an edge. This material is used often for hunting knives. The major drawback to this steel is that it has less chromium than other steels and consequently can rust. The heat treatment can be complex, and it moves slowly under the forging hammer.

A2 Steel - This is very tough steel that has less wear resistance than other tool steels. This steel is often used for custom combat knives because of its toughness. It has a carbon content range of 0.95-1.05%. This steel does not contain lots of chromium (typically around 5%) and needs to be maintained carefully to avoid rust. Knife blades will often be coated to avoid this issue.

CPM - "CPM" refers to the Crucible Particle Metallurgy process. This process results in a more homogenous mix of alloy elements within the steel, finer grain and overall better metallurgical properties.

CPM 10V Steel - This is one of the most wear-resistant tool steels. It also has decent toughness for a tool steel. This is a great choice if you are looking for something with lots of wear resistance but is not a really tough material.

CPM 3V Steel - This steel was designed to be tough while also sporting high wear resistance.

CPM M4 Steel - This steel has excellent wear resistance and toughness. It contains about 1.42% carbon.

D2 Steel - This steel has high chromium content, but less than what might classify as stainless steel. Because of this, it has some rust resistance. It is much tougher than most stainless steels, but not as tough as most of the other tool steel. D2 has excellent wear resistance. It has great edge retention but can be difficult to sharpen. This is also a challenging material to mirror polish, so you will almost never see it that way. Its carbon content is 1.50-1.60%.

L6 Steel - This steel is tough and holds an edge well. However, like other non-stainless steel, it rusts easily. Some consider this to be one of the best steels available for cutlery. It is also used frequently in saw blades, but any knife made from this material needs consistent maintenance.

M2 Steel - This steel is extremely heat resistant. It has about .85% carbon. It holds an edge really, really well, but it can be brittle on large knives.

O1 Steel - This material has good edge retention, because it is hard material. Its major problem is that it rusts rather quickly if it isn't maintained. It has a carbon content range of .85-1.00%.

W2 Steel - This steel is basically plain carbon steel with extra carbon. It is very hard and holds an edge well. Because of the overall lack of alloy elements, particularly manganese, it can be selectively hardened with clay or differential heat to create a hamon.

Stainless Steels

Stainless steel knives will have chromium as a significant alloy ingredient, typically at a minimum of 12-13%.

The 400 Series:

420 Steel – This has about

.38% carbon. The low carbon content means that 420 tends to be soft and doesn't hold an edge well. It is low-quality, low-cost material. Many cheap knives tend to be made of this material because of its cost. The blades need to be sharpened frequently, and often chip. On the bright side, all 420 stainless steel is extremely rust resistant. This means that one of the best uses for this material is to make diving knives.

440 Steel - There are three different types of 440 steel. The hardest part of telling them apart is that low-end makers often mark "440" on the tang of the blade and not the letter grade. This is especially true with lower grades, in hopes that the user will not know the difference. This has led certain knife manufacturers to rename 440C as other things in order to differentiate the quality of the product.

440A Steel – This steel has a carbon content range of .65-.75%. This is a low-cost stainless steel. It is typically used on low-end knives and does not have good edge retention due to lower hardness. It is the most rust resistant of 440 series steel.

440B Steel – This is very similar to 440A, but has a higher carbon content range (.75-.95%) and therefore higher overall hardness.

440C Steel - This has a carbon content range between .95-1.20%. This is considered a higher-end stainless steel. This alloy is one of the most common in production knives. It is wear resistant, and it is a hard steel. Many custom makers avoid 440C due to the confusion of customers when it comes to the quality of the other steels in the 440 series.

416 Steel - This is a non-hardening, stainless steel alloy commonly used for fittings such as guards, bolsters and liners. It's preferred by many custom makers.

154 CM Steel - This is a high-quality, stainless steel used by many production and custom makers. It has a carbon content of 1.05%. 154 CM holds an edge well and is hard. It actually has pretty good toughness for how hard the steel is, as well. It is tougher than 440 C. Some go as far as to call 154CM one of the first "super steels." The Japanese version is

called ATS-34 and the European version is RWL-34.

AEBL Steel – Among the least alloyed of stainless steels, AEBL performs like 1084 or 1095 when it comes to edge retention and ease of sharpening. It is a favorite of custom kitchen knife makers because of the combination of rust resistance and easy sharpening. Its fine grain size makes for good edge stability on thin edges

The AUS Series (Japanese Stainless Steel):

The biggest improvement of the AUS series over the 400 Series is the addition of vanadium, which improves wear resistance and gives good toughness. The AUS series is commonly used in production knives.

AUS-6 Steel – This has .65% carbon, and is a low-quality steel, comparable to 420.

AUS-8 Steel – Cold Steel made this steel, made from .75% carbon, popular. This is tough steel and holds an edge well.

AUS-10 Steel - This steel is comparable to 440C, and has 1.1% carbon. It contains more vanadium and less chromium than 440C, so it is slightly tougher, but also a little less rust resistant.

Bohler M390 Steel - This material is very stain resistant, has 1.9% carbon and sports excellent wear resistance. The addition of vanadium provides good hardness and wear resistance.

Bohler N680 Steel - This is another very hard steel, containing .54% carbon, which is highly stain resistant. It is good for saltwater applications.

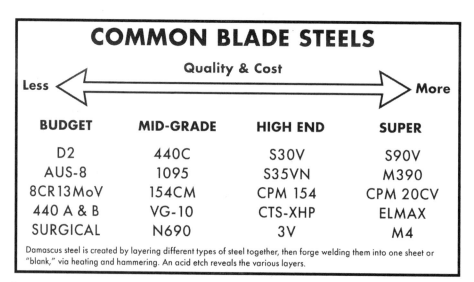

COMMON BLADE STEELS

Quality & Cost

Less ⟵—————————⟶ More

BUDGET	MID-GRADE	HIGH END	SUPER
D2	440C	S30V	S90V
AUS-8	1095	S35VN	M390
8CR13MoV	154CM	CPM 154	CPM 20CV
440 A & B	VG-10	CTS-XHP	ELMAX
SURGICAL	N690	3V	M4

Damascus steel is created by layering different types of steel together, then forge welding them into one sheet or "blank," via heating and hammering. An acid etch reveals the various layers.

Image courtesy of Knafs.com.

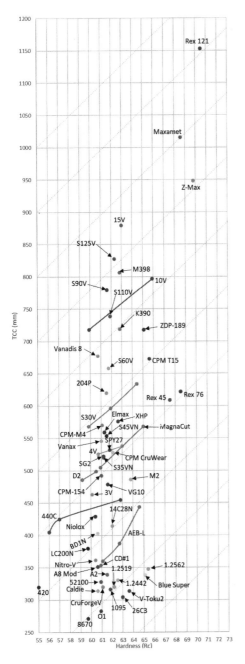

Image courtesy of Larrin Thomas/Knifesteelnerds.com.

N690 Steel - This steel is made in Austria is very similar to 440C, containing 1.07% carbon.

SXXV Series (CPM):

This series is becoming quite popular because of its strength, ability to resist rust and how well it holds an edge. These can be difficult steels to sharpen if you need to give them a new edge. All of these steels are very wear

---

The biggest improvement of the AUS series over the 400 Series is the addition of vanadium, which improves wear resistance and gives good toughness.

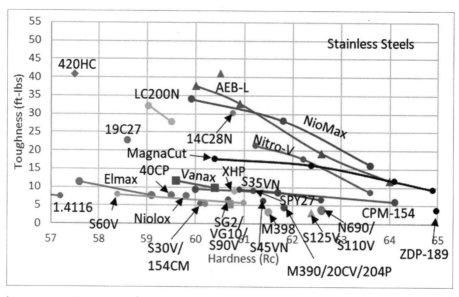

Image courtesy of Larrin Thomas/Knifesteelnerds.com.

resistant. These types are also very difficult to mirror polish, so you will almost never see a mirrored knife in these steels. The 30, 60 and 90 in this series stand for 3%, 6% and 9% vanadium in the alloy respectively.

S30V Steel – This is steel designed to be used in knives. This steel is very tough, and yet still has great wear resistance. For how tough the steel is, it actually has

very good hardness, which is why many consider it to be one of the best choices for knifemaking. It has a carbon content of 1.45%.

S60V Steel – S60V contains lots of vanadium and a carbon content of 2.15%, so it features high wear resistance. It is a step above S30V. Currently, this steel is not commonly used.

S90V Steel - This steel is defined by superior edge retention.

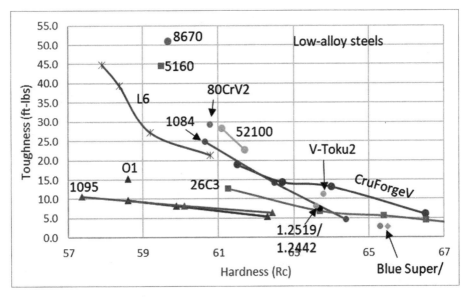

Image courtesy of Larrin Thomas/Knifesteelnerds.com.

However, it can be almost impossible to sharpen. Right now, custom makers are the only ones using this type of steel. Its carbon content is around 2.30%.

S35VN Steel- This close cousin of S30V contains additional Niobium to improve the sharpenability.

VG 10 Steel - Referred to as super steel, VG 10 is high-end stainless steel. Vanadium gives it extra toughness. This steel holds an edge really well. It is also very rust resistant, with a carbon content of 0.95-1.05%.

Want To Learn More?

For a deeper dive, look up Larrin Thomas' nifesteelnerds.com website and check out the article, *How to pick the best steel for every knife.* His book, *Knife Engineering*, is also essential. ▲

CHAPTER 9

A BUYER'S GUIDE TO DAMASCUS STEEL

One of the hot trends in today's market is the explosion in the art of pattern-welded or damascus steel. Those who would withstand the raindrops of skepticism and climb the ladder through the west Texas wind will find a dizzying mosaic of patterns by a not-so-random group of qualified smiths.

There are many "how to make damascus" articles and books out there, so let's take a different angle on this chapter. What does a knife buyer or collector need to know about damascus or pattern-welded steel?

The City In Syria?

First off, let's make sure we're using the same words in the same ways. Some would argue that the term "damascus" refers to an ancient technique from the Middle East, the details of which are now lost to modern knifemakers. Those people would be right in the strictest sense. The term "pattern welded" is more technically correct, as the art and skill of creating this steel involves multiple forge welds to make a pattern within a single block or billet of steel.

Technicalities aside, the label "damascus steel" has become the equivalent of "pattern welded" when it comes to the modern craft. For the sake of this chapter, when I say "damascus," I am referring to pattern-welded steel made by current and modern techniques.

"What Are Those Squiggly Lines On The Blade?"

One of the questions that knifemakers love to poke fun at comes from customers who have never read a chapter like this: "How do you get the lines on the steel like that?" In its simplest form, making damascus requires at least two types of steel with varying nickel content. The simpler carbon steels, particularly those with some manganese, make the dark lines. Steels with higher nickel content make the bright lines.

Among the most popular steel combinations include 1084 or 1095 welded with 15n20. Some variation of this combination is nearly a universal starting point for American-made damascus. Another quality option is the combination of O1 and L6.

In its simplest form, making damascus requires at least two types of steel with varying nickel content. The simpler carbon steels, particularly those with some manganese, make the dark lines. Steels with higher nickel content make the bright lines.

Each line in the final product represents a single piece of steel at the beginning of the process. To weld properly, each piece of bar stock for each layer must be ground clean. The contrasting layers are stacked and tack welded together into a billet, and then forge welded into a single piece through a variety of advanced smithing techniques.

To make each weld requires specialized equipment to achieve consistent quality. The maker needs a forge capable of more than 2,000 degrees Fahrenheit. The steel must then be hit or smashed in order for the welds to stick. While this may be accomplished by hand, most makers use a power hammer, a hydraulic press or both (each of which can cost as much as a used car).

Once the initial weld is set, the billet must be "drawn out," meaning lengthened and thinned, to prepare for re-stacking. The initial billet (let's say 10 layers for the sake of illustration), is cut into pieces, ground clean and re-stacked. If the original 10-layer billet is re-stacked in four pieces and welded, the layer count becomes 40 layers. After welding, drawing, restacking, and another four-layer weld, the billet is 160 layers, and so on.

Once the final layer count is reached, the pattern is manipulated by twisting, grinding or pressing, and then drawn out into a final billet for stock removal or forged into the final shape of the intended knife.

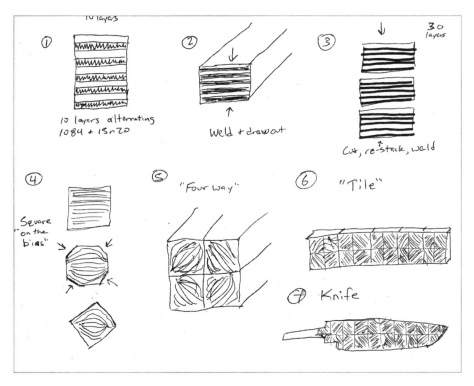

In these diagrams, you can see the basic procedure to make an explosion pattern billet. This pattern is "simple," requiring only four welds. In my shop with a power hammer, it would take me more than half a day to move through these steps. My goal here isn't to teach you how to make damascus, but for you as a buyer to appreciate the amount of work and skill that goes into every billet.

If you think that sounds complicated, hang on, because that's the simplest version. A billet may be welded with the layers flat or vertical. It may be flipped, rounded and re-squared, or stacked in an unlimited number of variable orders. Complex patterns may be squared and then welded in a "four way" or even a nine-way stack. Patterns that are four-wayed typically reveal the pattern on the end cuts, not the sides of the billet, which requires a difficult "tile weld."

I haven't even mentioned multi-bar twist patterns that include four or more billets twisted and welded together. Don't forget the various canister and powder patterns, or the wire-EDM patterns that create everything from scary faces to wild animals in the billet. At the cutting edge of damascus technology, some knifemakers are now experimenting with pattern manipulation through the use of a 3D printer.

My point in glossing over the complexity of high-end damascus is simply this: it's dang complicated to produce some of these patterns. Much like, "How much does a plumber cost?" the answer to "Why is damascus so expensive?" has everything to do with the amount of skilled labor and professional equipment involved. More complexity equals more time equals a higher price tag. When a maker looks you in the eye and says, "$5,000," when you inquire about a mosaic damascus bowie, take their word for it that they've put in the time and labor to justify the price.

As another way to compare, consider that a maker constructs a pair of identical knives, one in 1084 and another in a mosaic damascus pattern. If the 1084 knife sells for $1,000, and the mosaic piece took an additional four days work to forge the damascus, what should the damascus knife sell for? Depending on the maker's shop rate, the damascus piece could be easily $3,000.

How To Get What You Want

You may come to the point where you want to custom order

a damascus knife direct from the maker. First, you won't get what you don't ask for. If you have expectations for a certain pattern, you need to make those expectations clear. At the same time, you're the customer and not typically the artist. Some of the best work will come from giving the maker latitude on the design and the pattern.

As a maker, I appreciate a general idea to work toward, such as "an explosion pattern bowie." I personally don't like too many specifics, such as, "an explosion pattern bowie with 36 layers per corner, and four full explosion patterns on the blade."

Another consideration is that a high-end knife is more than just the blade. If you're going to pay

> ... a high-end knife is more than just the blade. If you're going to pay for damascus, you should be prepared for an equal quality handle material.

for damascus, you should be prepared for an equal quality handle material. Don't ask a maker for $1,000 worth of damascus on a knife with $20 micarta scales. If you want ivory, stag or burl wood, it's OK to say so.

As a final word about commissioning damascus pieces, I ask you to be considerate of the maker's time. To start from nothing and end up with a mosaic knife takes a long time. You order steel, then wait for it to arrive. You prep billets, then work in a forge welding day or two into your workflow. Once the steel is welded, you've

---

When you buy a high-end damascus knife, you are getting the work of a skilled domestic craftsman, whose reputation will vouch for their quality, and whose steel composition will be verifiable. On the other hand, when you buy a cheap damascus knife, you can pretty well guess that it was made in Asia, most often Pakistan.

got a day to grind and heat treat. Add a few more days for blade finishing, another day or two for handle work, and a day or two for the sheath.

If you're dealing with a reputable maker, they'll give you a fair estimate of when the knife will be delivered, but don't be surprised if the answer is "sometime next year." If you ask a maker at Thanksgiving for a damascus knife for a Christmas gift, the answer is probably going to be "no."

What About Those Gun Show Knives?

I would be remiss if I didn't mention the damascus knives found cheaply at gun shows everywhere. And you'd be remiss if you didn't ask "What's the difference?" or

"Why do those damascus knives cost only $100?"

When you buy a high-end damascus knife, you are getting the work of a skilled domestic craftsman, whose reputation will vouch for their quality, and whose steel composition will be verifiable. On the other hand, when you buy a cheap damascus knife, you can pretty well guess that it was made in Asia, most often Pakistan. While the craftsmen there have mastered the rudiments of pattern welding, what they can't guarantee is the composition of their steel. Any two steels of varying nickel content will make a pattern, but there is no guarantee that those two steels are hardenable to acceptable standards. Tuna cans and car bumpers may make a pattern, but they won't make a good knife. As technology improves, so does the quality of the deception. There are now imported knives turning up on the gun show circuit and online that are a single steel with laser engraved patterns being sold as "damascus." That's a cool and innovative way to make a pattern on a blade, for sure. It's also sure as heck not damascus.

When it comes to damascus steel, you absolutely get what you pay for. Unknown steel welded in unknown conditions by sweatshop laborers just isn't the same as the damascus you'd get from a local craftsman.

A word of caution: "those folks" know to say that their steel is 1095 and 15n20, but the performance of

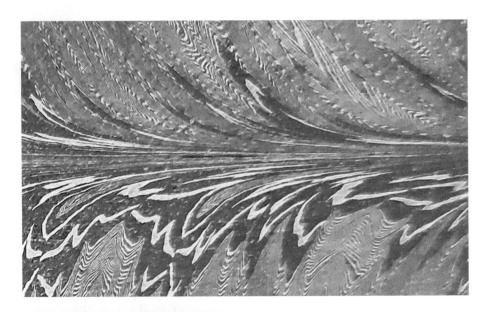

These damascus blades didn't turn out so great. Can you tell why?

their steel would seem to indicate otherwise. If the price seems too good to be true, there's your sign.

Stainless Damascus

A handful of reputable American smiths make high-quality, pattern-welded steel in stainless. The process of welding stainless steel is a level of skill and complexity beyond the welding of carbon steels. Unless you're hearing of stainless damascus from a small and select group of makers, you

On the left-hand picture, decarb shows through the final etch as a gray blotchy area. On the right-hand picture, the issue is corrected after grinding away more steel, re-polishing and re-etching.

had better do your homework.

The Swedish company Damasteel also produces high-quality, stainless damascus in a variety of complex patterns. Its product is top of the line.

Damascus Problems To Look For

Aside from the fundamental qualification of starting with quality steel, there are a few other areas to examine that are unique to the damascus knife. High-quality damascus should have no visible weld seams or "cold shuts." These will appear as dark or rough lines in between otherwise solid sections of steel.

The accompanying pictures show blades that the makers rejected due to bad welds. Look at the dark lines on the ricasso of the folding knife blade. On the feather pattern, there's a weld inclusion right down the center. That feather pattern billet had to be forge welded and re-stacked at least 8 times prior to the weld that failed. Everyone who has ever made damascus has ruined billets, and even an expert has a bad weld now and then.

Damascus requires special treatment called "etching" to show the contrast between the layers. Several problems can show up in the etching process that don't apply to monosteel knives. Cloudy or splotchy areas in the contrast can be the result of "decarb," areas where the extreme heat of the forging process has changed the steel composition slightly. Splotches can also be the result of uneven etching, where the blade was not 100% clean prior to going into the etching solution.

There are times that a perfectly polished surface, even at 800+ grit hand sanded, looks perfect until the etch. After the etch, the decarb at the bottom of the original heavy grit scratches can show up. It will look a lot like a poor polish left underlying scratches, but instead it'll be a perfectly smooth area of uneven contrast.

Damascus Is Worth It

Damascus steel presents unique challenges to the maker, but also unique value to the buyer. When you buy damascus straight from the craftsman, you can expect to pay well for it, but you will have a one-of-a-kind demonstration of the height of bladesmithing skills. The prize is worth the cost! ▲

CHAPTER 10

CARING FOR YOUR COLLECTION

Jesus warned his followers in Matthew 6:19 that our earthly treasures are at risk of being destroyed by "moth and rust," and are in danger from "thieves who break in and steal." While I'd be plenty scared of the moth that could destroy a knife, it's that sneaky devil of rust and corrosion that the knife collector fights more often.

The care and maintenance of your collection is critical to maintaining its value and usefulness over time.

Keep It Clean

A clean knife is a good knife. A dirty knife is a knife at risk. That sounds simple enough, but if you've read up on this subject, you'll see opinions all over the place. To help you break down some pros and cons, here's a comparative chart.

The basic cleaning procedure is to put some of your chosen cleaner on a cloth and wipe down the knife. Some prefer a cotton cloth (I like old T-shirts), while others prefer microfiber cloths. Whatever

CLEANER	PROS	CONS	COMMENTS
Dish soap and water	•easily available •mild, not harmful •does the job well	•includes water, and so requires drying to not rust	No soaking in the sink. No dishwasher, EVER!
WD40	•easily available •does the job •displaces water	•smelly •evaporates over time	Short term protection
Acetone or denatured alcohol	•cleans grease, glue •strips oil, wax	•mildly toxic •can harm handle finishes	Great for tape residue or sticky messes.
Polishing paste such as Simichrome or Flitz	•mildly abrasive •good for rust or discoloration •great for bolsters	•can mar mirror finishes •can discolor blade coatings	Best cleaner type for light rust.

cloth you choose, use it only a few times. If your cloth gets contaminated with any kind of dirt or grit, throw it out or you'll risk scratching your knives as you clean.

A knife should be cleaned before it's put into storage, and after every time that it is handled. If you've been to a knife show, you'll know that simple handling can put spit drops and fingerprints on a knife. If left unclean, these can lead to rust or discoloration within a matter of hours or days. If you get your knives out to show your friends, wipe the knives down before you put them away.

Use Protection

There are two main categories of knife protectants: oil and wax.

When choosing an oil, I find 3-in-1, mineral oil or gun oil work just fine. I like to put a little on a rag and rub it on for longer term storage. For short-term protection, I'll put a drop on the blade and rub it around. When it comes to folding knives, I prefer an oil with Teflon for the joints. Don't over-oil a pivot, and don't use too thick of an oil as that'll be more likely to collect gunk.

The downside to oil is that it can capture dust or grit that can harm your knife in handling. Another downside is that some oils get sticky over time and may be hard to clean up later.

Renaissance Wax has long been the wax of choice for knife care. "Ren Wax" is a clear, museum-grade wax that comes in a little, white can. It's safe for long-term use, and safe on both blade and handle material. On a clean

The downside to oil is that it can capture dust or grit that can harm your knife in handling. Another downside is that some oils get sticky over time and may be hard to clean up later.

knife, wipe on a thin coat, let it dry and then wipe it off. Most people recommend two or three coats for full protection. After that, add a light coat of oil if you're so inclined.

Although Ren Wax is the industry standard, there are some other good wax options out there as well. One advantage to wax is that the knife's shine can be restored with a simple buff with a soft cloth. It also makes the grain in a wood handle really "pop!"

One special preservation technique worth mentioning involves oil and natural handle materials like bone, stag and ivory. While they'll do very well with a standard wax-then-oil type protection, some knifemakers that I trust recommend soaking or heavy coating in mineral oil for these materials.

These natural materials are susceptible to changes in size due to the humidity in the air, and the oil soak fills the spaces in the material so that the moisture makes less of an impact. When handle material is less likely to move with temperature or humidity, it is less likely to crack.

Knife Storage

At one extreme, you've got guys like me who accumulate user knives and end up with a "collection" of knives spread out all over the place in drawers, boxes, closets and backpacks. On the other side are folks like Lloyd Hale's patron, Owsley Brown Frazier, who end up having to build a whole freestanding museum to house their collection. Between those two extremes, however, are quite a few good options.

I've seen examples of nice display cases built specifically for knife collections. Some are vertical, some horizontal and others are wall mounted. A standard shadowbox makes a great display. One drawback to these kinds of arrangements has to do with light. Any time that your knife is exposed to light from one side only, the handle material may discolor on the exposed side.

If your knife comes with a stand, or a stand can be built, a custom knife makes a nice addition to a bookcase, shelf or mantle. I dream about a library-style man cave with taxidermy on one side, a giant desk, and shelves filled with books and knives.

One common way to store a large number of knives is a knife roll. Rolls are most often used to store kitchen cutlery or pocketknives, but may be adapted to other styles of knives as well. A good knife roll will have multiple pockets to keep the knives from bumping into each other. It will

---

Many collectors rightly view their knives as an investment or as valuable and worthy of protection. A safe or a safe deposit box is the way to go for these folks.

be made of durable material that will not hold moisture. It may also have a good handle for carrying and secure fasteners to keep it from unrolling.

Many collectors rightly view their knives as an investment or as valuable and worthy of protection. A safe or a safe deposit box is the way to go for these folks. The security is an upside, as is the controlled environment with limited light, limited humidity and consistent temperature. A downside is that it requires extra effort to share the collection with others, if that's your thing.

There are a few storage scenarios that are not good and may result in damage to your knives. Often repeated but often ignored is the admonition not to store a knife in its sheath. Leather holds moisture, and moisture contributes to corrosion or rust. While putting a knife in the sheath isn't a guaranteed disaster, it's also not a good long-term solution. I mentioned differential light already. While the idea of a beam of sunlight coming from heaven and highlighting your prize might be visually appealing, the UV in sunlight can cause discoloration of the exposed parts. Micarta and cocobolo are two materials that are especially susceptible, as well as any of the dyed woods.

If you're a hunter or a user-collector, it's tempting to leave your knife in your vehicle. While this is a great idea when it comes to utility and there-when-you-need-it, it's a bad idea for your knife. The

Shane's knives and sheaths took a beating from the elements inside that "watertight" container.

temperature swings of a vehicle can challenge the stability of your handle material, and a knife on the dashboard may get so hot as to compromise the integrity of the glue.

As a what-not-to-do story, my good friend and user-collector Shane had his hunting knives stored carefully in a "watertight" plastic tote underneath a "watertight" bed cover. The knives rode in the back of the truck in the rain on the way home from a deer hunt at the end of the season. The next fall, when Shane got out his knife tote for a pre-season sharpening session, he discovered that the tote wasn't so watertight after all. Water had made its way inside, and at least five of his customs were covered in rust and the sheaths full of mold. He ultimately sent the knives back to the makers for rehab, but even we weren't able to restore them to their original condition.

Collection Maintenance

Some of us are fairly into doing what we like to do, but not into maintenance schedules and record keeping. Even so, your collection would benefit from a little bit of both. You need to know your collection and be aware of its needs.

If you collect stainless or coated folding knives, maybe you don't need an aggressive wipe-down schedule. On the other hand, if you collect forged bowies, you had better keep them waxed or oiled regularly. If you use your customs for deer skinning, maybe a beginning- and end-of-season routine is enough. If you have customs in the kitchen, you'd better treat them right after every single use, as one incident of neglect in that environment can be detrimental. If you live in Arizona, you may not have to worry much about humidity, and so your maintenance schedule may be different than the collector with a beachfront home in Florida.

I consider record keeping as part of collection maintenance. If you've just got a few and you like to use them frequently, maybe mental notes are enough. On the other hand, as your collection grows in quantity, quality and value, record keeping becomes more important. Will you remember every single knife, when you got it, what it's made from, and what you paid? If you can, you're better than most people. Whether you go with a manual ledger or an electronic spreadsheet, as your collection grows it becomes important to keep good records. Pictures are an important part of the record as well.

There are two main reasons to keep good records. First, a detailed record is important if you intend to pass on your collection. Often, dad's "treasures" end up being sold or distributed. A detailed ledger makes for an honest sale and fair distribution.

One of the most common questions received by *BLADE* magazine employees is about how much an inherited collection is worth and how best to sell it. Do not expect those who follow you to know as much as you do

---

If you collect stainless or coated folding knives, maybe you don't need an aggressive wipe-down schedule. On the other hand, if you collect forged bowies, you had better keep them waxed or oiled regularly.

about your collection. Leave them a good record.

I've talked about "moth and rust," but left out the "thieves who break in and steal." The second reason to maintain good records involves replacement in the event of a theft, fire or flood. Police and insurance adjusters alike are not likely to be fluent in knife identification and appraisal. Further complicating that, knives don't have serial numbers that can be tracked like firearms. The quality of your insurance payout and the likelihood of police recovery both increase in magnitude equal to the quality of your record.

Speaking of insurance, there are several ways to insure your collection depending on its overall value. Many people assume their homeowner's or renter's insurance covers their knives, and this may be true to an extent. Any coverage under this kind of insurance will likely be subject to a deductible that is a percentage of your overall property value, and there is likely to be a limit to the coverage. Ask your insurance agent for the details of your specific policy coverage. Many times, they can also offer a "rider," an extra fee on the main policy that will cover the increased value of collectibles or that may lower the deductible.

If you find that the specifics or limitations of your existing insurance don't cover you well, there are companies that specialize in insuring collectibles. If you keep good records, these companies will replace your items if they are lost, stolen, or destroyed by fire or flood. Collectors who routinely ship expensive knives often use this coverage in lieu of the coverage offered by the delivery services, as a collector policy will cover knives in transit.

Don't forget that protection starts with you. Most people don't get into collecting because they enjoy cleaning, waxing or oiling knives. Even so, collection maintenance is critical if you want your knives to be ready to use or clean and beautiful. Well-maintained knives are more likely to maintain their value. ▲

CHAPTER 11

AN AMERICAN CASE STUDY

When it comes to a chapter on collecting factory production knives, I needed a good case study to flesh out the basic ideas. A *case* study. How about a Case study?

W.R. Case and Sons, or more commonly called Case Knives, is perhaps *the* classic American knife manufacturer. To explore the company and collecting, I spoke with Fred Feightner, marketing manager; and Jonathan Bradish, community manager, Case Collectors Club and event marketing. Each of these men has been with Case for 18 years as of this writing, and they're both well versed in what Case has to offer. They live and work in Bradford, Pennsylvania, the home of the company since 1905.

The Case Story

The story of Case knives begins back in 1889, when four enterprising brothers—William Russell (W.R.), Jean, John, and Andrew Case (a.k.a. "The Case Brothers")—began selling handcrafted knives from the back of a wagon in upstate New York.

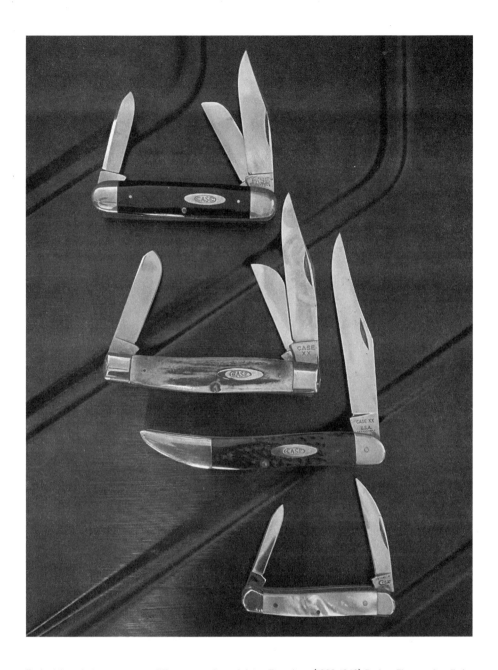

Each of these knives represents different eras. At top left is a Tested era (1920-1940) Barlow. The stag-handled Stockman below that is from the 1940-64 era. The Medium Toothpick below that is a "10-dot" from the 1970s. This was the first year Case committed to stamping knives to show the actual year that the knife was made. These are prized collectibles in the knife trade. Last, but not least, is Fred's own Mini Copperhead with a genuine mother-of-pearl handle from 2014. (Image courtesy of Case)

W.R.'s son, John Russell "Russ" Case, was the chief salesman, and sold the companies' knives out of a wagon along the roads in New York. Russ soon figured out he made more money buying and selling knives than his uncles did manufacturing them.

In 1902, Russ then formed W.R. Case & Sons, as it is known today. In 1905, they moved from upstate New York down to Pennsylvania. Now on its third factory site, the company continues to manufacture Case knives in Bradford.

Shortly after the move, W.R. purchased the family company's "XX" trademark. The XX and "Tested" brands were key to the company's early survival and growth.

Famous Case Knives

The company's journey continued with knife production for the United States military during both World Wars. Among the most famous of Case's wartime production is the V42 Special Forces dagger.

Produced toward the end of World War II for use by the newly formed Special Forces, the V42 was well liked and well received. Fortunately for the world (but perhaps unfortunately for Case), the war ended soon afterward, and the need for a Special Forces dagger waned. In all, there were only around 1,750 of these knives made before production ceased.

Although Case produced a replica from 1989 through 1993, the

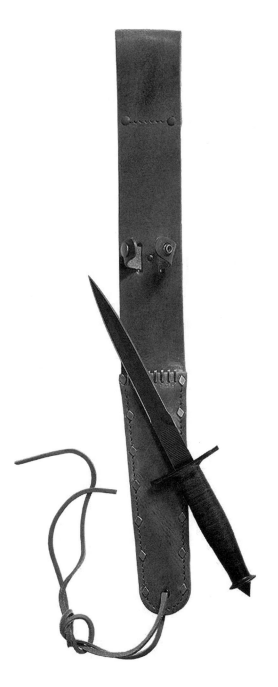

original V42 remains among the "holy grails" of Case collectors. An original V42, if you can ever find one for sale, will likely run you north of $5,000. The Case replicas typically sell for more than $500. Not bad!

President Dwight Eisenhower was quite a Case knives fan. He and his wife Mamie would mail in a factory order every year for many years. They used these knives to give to friends and visiting dignitaries. When was the last time you heard of a president carrying

The Case V42 is one of the most collectible knives on the market. If you're lucky enough to stumble across one, don't pass it up! (Image courtesy of Case)

a knife, much less gifting one? I can just imagine the scene: "Hello and welcome, Prime Minister, here is a Case knife. You'll need this to get the full American experience!"

Case knives won the NASA contract to make the knives for the astronauts of the Gemini and Apollo missions. One of the challenges was the requirement for an "inert" handle material. Case went down the street to a local bread company and melted down plastic bread bags for one of the earliest prototypes, although aluminum was the final choice for the production handle.

The knives were kept either in a scabbard fastened by the door, or in an equipment rucksack. While it might sound far-fetched that the astronauts would need a knife to fight off aliens or open space mail, the real purpose of the knife on the mission was to be there as a survival tool if something went wrong either in space or after re-entry. Imagine, you go all the way to the moon, then crash your

> One of the most popular Case models for both users and collectors is the two-blade trapper. The pattern evolved in the early part of the 20th century out of the older two-blade jack knife patterns.

Case knives have gone to the moon and back—literally. Apollo astronauts needed a knife for Earth, not the moon, upon return from outer space. (Image courtesy of Case)

spaceship on a deserted island when you try to come home. You might need a knife!

There was a Case knife in the Apollo 11 lunar lander, although it didn't get out to spread the mayo at the first moon picnic.

Overall, there were nine Case knives that made a trip to the moon, including one currently on display at the Smithsonian. Case did a re-issue of the astronaut knife in 2019 to commemorate 50 years since the first moon landing.

Case knives are not just for presidents and astronauts. Case built many kinds of knives over its history, including a line of kitchen cutlery and specialized slaughterhouse and butchering knives. Case's current lineup of traditional knives includes its traditional folding knives, leather-handled fixed blades and a kitchen set. Case has recently drawn attention with its modern everyday carry knives, the Marilla and the Kinzua. These are named after recreational areas in the Bradford area. The Marilla is a flipper folder and was the "American Knife of the Year" at Blade Show 2021.

Collect The History

Fred and Jon had different answers when it comes to the question of "Why should I collect Case knives?"

Fred leaned into the history and craftsmanship. He said, "Case is a classic, American company. Every knife is made with hand work, by real people in Pennsylvania. You can't just find that anywhere. We've been around so long that we honestly believe we've built the perfect knife for everybody at one time or another. When you buy a Case knife, you join in with a long history of knife users and collectors. You can buy the knife your great grandpa carried."

One thing that has contributed to the collectability of Case knives over the years is the dot dating system. While it's beyond the scope here to go into great detail, since 1970, each Case knife has been marked with a code that shows what year it was manufactured. Rather than simply guessing on a date range based on a mark, for the past 52 years you can nail down the manufacture to a specific year. That opens up collecting for your birth year, your favorite decade or even one from every manufacturing year. The date code lets you know exactly what you're looking for.

One of the most popular Case models for both users and collectors is the two-blade trapper. The pattern evolved in the early part of the 20th century out of the older two-blade jack knife patterns. The trapper pattern features a long clip blade for detail work and a large spey blade for skinning.

Ultimately, there are dozens of patterns including stockman, peanut, sowbelly and many others. It's good practice to find a pattern you like and dive in. Whether you use them or just accumulate, there are plenty of variations in materials and patterns.

While focusing on a single pattern is a great way to start a collection of Case knives, or any other production knife for that matter, that's not the only approach. Maybe you'd prefer to collect only knives in your favorite color. You could buy every knife that Case has made in blue jigged bone. Or maybe you want to buy every knife the brand made in your birth year. Maybe you want to collect a certain rare handle material, like pearl, abalone or Sambar stag.

Join The Club

"Since 1981, Case operates a

well-established and organized Case Collectors Club [CCC]," Jon said. "We started with 426 charter members, and now have a membership of thousands. We offer our CCC members a complete yearly catalog for free. We have a quarterly magazine that includes articles on new products, stories of Case history and historical knives, media events and even a junior section that features kids' games. We also offer our club exclusive access to promotional knives and a members-only internet forum for active talk, swap and trade."

The CCC also has limited edition knives manufactured exclusively for its members. That's a common collecting strategy. Case produces various limited editions where each knife in the series is numbered and the overall production remains low, around 3,000 pieces or less. The CCC knives are another limited run product.

Another way that Case produces limited runs is with collaborative series. The most recent collaborations were designed by legendary custom knifemaker Tony Bose. Case produced limited run knives in some of Tony's most well-known patterns, including the "Lanny's Clip" and "Back Pocket."

Buying Case Knives

If you want to buy a Case knife, you can buy one directly from the factory. Case also has an extensive dealer network. If you see an advertised "Authorized Dealer," you can know with confidence that this sales outlet has partnered with Case directly for distribution.

Those who carry the label of "Master Dealer" have a commitment to carry the entire Case product line. If there's any current knife that Case makes, your nearest Master Dealer will be able to work with you to get it.

Other than its official dealer network and company channels, Jon and Fred pointed out that eBay remains one of the best places to purchase vintage Case knives if you're not a member of the CCC forums. The All About Pocketknives forums have a good group of vintage Case enthusiasts as well. There are many, many books written about Case knives and Case collecting. The company has a YouTube channel as well as Instagram, Facebook and Twitter.

Whether you're after a knife to skin a deer or open your mail, or whether you intend to be a small-time buyer or amass a huge collection, you can't go wrong with a knife from W.R. Case and Sons. It's a great entry into the world of knife collecting. ▲

CHAPTER 12

STARTING FROM THE TOPS

Another on-ramp for new collectors is TOPS Knives. It's a great example of a brand creating an atmosphere perfect for collecting.

Imagine you're a soldier, stranded on the side of a cliff, bad guys above and below. You've got your knife wedged in a crack in the rock, and you're hanging onto the handle. If there was ever a time for your knife to be unbreakable, now would be a good time. Service men and women all over the world depend on a knife in scenarios far more dangerous than this one. An unbreakable knife is more than just a convenience.

History

TOPS Knives was founded in 1998 by Michael Fuller, Special Forces veteran. His initial goal was to make unbreakable knives for warfighters. Beginning with the original Steel Eagle model, TOPS became popular with the tactical knife crowd. In addition to fighting and survival knives, TOPS now has over 250 active models including everyday carry, hunting, bushcraft and utility models.

Current owner Leo Espinoza has been with the company since nearly the beginning. He's done "all of the jobs" that go along with manufacturing TOPS knives. He is

Some collectors focus on origin, such as knives made in the United States. TOPS uses American materials and labor for all its products. (Image courtesy of TOPS.)

responsible for the majority of the new model design work.

From the beginning, TOPS has been a small home-grown company with a family atmosphere. Located in Idaho Falls, Idaho, TOPS employs locals and is a great place to work. TOPS uses all-American materials, including some from Idaho. TOPS knives are 100% American, by American workers to meet American quality expectations.

One attribute to the company that makes TOPS knives interesting and collectible is the sheer variety of models. It focuses on fixed blade knives, although they do have a few folder models as well. If you want an axe, a sword, a hatchet, a bowie, an everyday carry knife, a hunting knife or just

The Tom Brown Tracker is one of the most popular knives TOPS produces. (Image courtesy of TOPS)

about any other fixed blade you can think of, TOPS has a model in its lineup. Some of their more popular models are the Brothers of Bushcraft Fieldcraft, Tom Brown Tracker and the later models of the original Steel Eagle.

Steels

Another distinctive thing about TOPS knives is its consistent use of 1095 carbon steel. While there are other steels used in a few knives (154CM, N690CO, S35VN), differentially heat treated 1095 is "their thing."

Another distinctive thing about TOPS knives is its consistent use of 1095 carbon steel. While there are other steels used in a few knives (154CM, N690CO, S35VN), differentially heat treated 1095 is "their thing."

As a knifemaker, I was skeptical. I know from experience that 1095 can be tricky to harden. After talking to the folks at TOPS, I have full confidence in their work. The reason why has a name: Benny Carbajal. Since the beginning of TOPS' manufacturing, Benny performed all the heat treating. That adds up to well over 100,000 knives.

While I know I'm right not to suggest differentially heat treating 1095 to a beginning knifemaker, I have no doubt that Benny gets it right consistently after 100,000 tries.

By the way, a "differential heat treat" is a method that hardens the cutting edge while leaving the back of the knife "soft." The primary advantage of this method is that it increases the toughness of the knife. Hard steel is brittle, while softer steel is tough. By hardening the edge only, TOPS knives can maintain a good edge that's easy to sharpen, while at the same time retaining the high toughness that makes a knife "unbreakable."

There's a real-world story about a U.S. Army chaplain in Afghanistan who carried a TOPS Tom Brown Tracker while deployed. He lost the knife in a small village, but the knife was his favorite. Later, on a return trip, he asked around among the villagers. Eventually, he found the woman who was in possession of his knife. She had been using the knife to split firewood by hammering on the spine with a steel pipe—something referred to as "batoning." The saw teeth of the Tracker were mushroomed out and blunt, but the edge of the knife was able to be restored. This kind of performance—or the survival of this kind of abuse—is a result of the differential heat treat process.

Handles

Another thing TOPS knives are known for is "The X" handles. TOPS mostly uses layered synthetic handle materials, like Micarta and G10. The handles are cut and ground by CNC machines before being assembled and shaped by Benny. The contour of the handles combined with the layered material makes an X pattern on the handle of many different TOPS designs.

Tops On The Screen

TOPS knives have made plenty of appearances on the hips of famous people, and are often seen on TV and in the movies. They're popular among the competitors on *Naked and Afraid*. Pro wrestler The Undertaker carried one in public. The Tom Brown Tracker is featured prominently in the movie *The Hunted*, starring Benicio Del Toro and Tommy Lee Jones. TOPS started production of the Tracker around the time of the movie's filming.

A Regular At Knife Shows

Another thing that sets TOPS apart is its dedication and openness to interacting with collectors. TOPS is a regular table holder at knife shows all over the country, which means you're never too far from meeting the makers and designers. There's no substitute for an in-person experience, especially when it comes to collecting knives. ▲

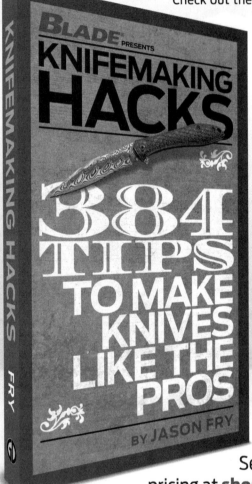